MINISTRY AND MUSIC

Robert H. Mitchell

The Westminster Press
Philadelphia

Published by The Westminster Press ®
Philadelphia, Pennsylvania

Printed in the United States of America

9 8 7 6 5 4 3

Library of Congress Cataloging in Publication Data

Mitchell, Robert H   1921–
    Ministry and music.

    Includes bibliographical references.
    1. Church music—Protestant Churches. II. Title.
ML3100.M55   264'.2   77–20815
ISBN 0–664–24186–7

Contents

Preface

This book was written because pastors are different from church musicians. Minister and musician may be expected to have (1) different preparation, (2) different views and objectives concerning ministry and music, and (3) difficulty in identifying the nature of the difference. This is an attempt to identify common ground where the Biblical/theological orientation of the pastor can meet the musical expertise of the musician. It is an attempt to clarify a number of positions, not necessarily a "right" one, in relationship to various church music functions. The purpose, then, is that conversation, understanding, and growth may take place between pastor and musician.

This is not a book on how to organize and direct a volunteer church choir, how to play the organ, or how to lead congregational singing. Occasionally specific illustrations and suggestions of such things have been included. These are meant primarily for the pastor as tangible illustrations of what might otherwise be rather vague concepts. Secondarily, they are included to serve as suggestions for the church musician.

My own professional experience has been divided between ministry in the parish church, including the developing of large graded choir programs, and in the theological seminary—at California Baptist Seminary, Covina, California, as professor of church music, and presently at American Baptist Seminary of the West, Berkeley, California, as professor of church and the arts. This teaching role has involved countless conferences with pastors and church musicians, both in individual and group situations. From these conferences the matters dealt with in this book have emerged. Through this process, two basic conclusions about music and ministry arise. First, the good news can only be meaningfully proclaimed by a staff of persons who demonstrate in their relationship with one another what it means to attempt to live by the gospel. The second is that "living by the gospel" is most important in dealing with differing understandings of the church. It is not essential that we agree on all matters of faith and practice. It is essential that we learn to handle lack of agreement in a Christian manner. Differences of understanding should not be concealed or ignored. They should be identified and explored in order that mutual growth may take place.

My parish and educational ministry has been within the free-church (Baptist and Presbyterian) tradition. It is from this stance that I have addressed the issues. For most issues this makes little difference. Occasionally a reader from that segment of the church which identifies itself as "liturgical" will need to question what is said and evaluate it in terms of a different background.

Chapter 7 of this book is based on my article on acoustics published in the July/August, 1967, issue of *Your Church;* and material from this article is used with the permission of the publisher.

Finally, it will be noted that a remarkable number of citations refer to books by Dr. Erik Routley, previously of Great Britain and now of Princeton, New Jersey. This is appropriate because no one else in the twentieth century has written as profusely, as widely, and as competently concerning the church and its music. I acknowledge my enormous debt to his scholarship and his provocative thinking. No one else has so influenced my understanding of the church, the nature of its music and worship, and the clarification that such understanding can bring to one's concept of the gospel and the whole of Christian living. I invite you to share this acquaintanceship as you discover and read any of Dr. Routley's books dealing with the church's hymnody, the history of its music, and the theological implications of its worship and music, both past and present.

                                                         R.H.M.

Berkeley, California

One

MINISTRY
AND CHURCH MUSIC

This is a nonmusical book about church music. It is neither a development of a theology of church music nor a handbook for its administration. Rather, it is an attempt to comment on some of the important functional aspects of music in the church from a theological standpoint in a way that is intelligible to the nonmusician. It seeks to identify common ground where the professional musician and the professional theologian may converse, learn from and inform each other, and share the experience of relationship and growth to which the gospel invites us all. The assumptions behind this book are expressed in the following six statements.

1. Every pastor can expect to be involved in church music.

It is most unlikely that a pastor will escape involvement in music. Perhaps 20 percent to 25 percent of most general church meetings will be given over to music. The pastor can expect to be responsible for coordinating and guiding staff musicians. He or she may be part of the decision-making process leading to the choice of a new hymnal, an organ, or the building of a new sanctuary.

The pastor will inevitably participate in the evaluation of the musical activities of the church and in choosing persons to lead such activities. He or she may actually be involved in the musical leadership of the congregation, and will certainly plan and lead worship services that include music.

2. Every church musician can normally expect to be involved in ministry.

A distinction can be made between making music in church and the carrying out of its ministry. *Ministry* has to do with things that happen in the lives of persons. That's what the church is all about. On the other hand, it is possible for music-making to exist as the pursuit of aesthetic goals or as the perfunctory carrying out of routine liturgical tasks. When either of these becomes the objective, whether consciously or unconsciously, it is easily possible for the functional goal of the whole process to become *music* rather than ministry. It is the responsibility of the church musician to recognize this distinction and to expect and accept the priority of ministry.

3. A pastor should be able to relate theology to the goals and practices of music.

Involved here is the role of the pastor—the appropriate expectation of his or her particular competence. Some nineteenth-century concepts of this role, fortunately less common today, viewed the pastor as "ultimate authority," "voice of God," "ruler of his church." Today one often hears this role described as "enabler," "energizer," or "resource person." Whichever of these concepts one prefers, it is appropriate to expect a certain expertise in a pastor as a result of graduate professional seminary study. One basic aspect of this expected competence includes Biblical studies and theology. The pastor should be an "expert" in this field. Unfortunately, within free-church theological education little or no attention is given to developing a theology of church music. The pastor's three or four years of preparation for ministry in the seminary may have included virtually no important training or experience in the field of music.

Since the Reformation there has been very little theologizing about music and the arts in the Protestant Church. More has been attempted in this direction since the middle of the twentieth century than in the previous four hundred years. As a result of this neglect, church music has remained outside of thoughtful systematic theological consideration. Thus, within Protestantism, neither experience nor tradition has nurtured the development of a Biblical/theological understanding of the church's music. Because of this the typical pastor must make a particular effort, often a creative one, to be able to relate this part of ministry to the larger system of theological understanding.

If a pastor is asked to state some theological guideline concerning this ever-present church music, it will probably be something like this: "Only the best music is appropriate for the worship of God." Such a concept sounds well, but, if unexamined, it eliminates the need for any further thought about the matter. It is then appropriate to press a bit further. Ask, "What do you mean by 'best'?" Are the criteria to be aesthetic, historical, emotional, or pragmatic? Or is it possible that they may be none of these but rather the simple preference of what the pastor knows and likes? Wherever the answer lies, there is no question but that the pastor will be making value judgments in the area of music. Anytime a choice is made, some kind of value system is in operation. It is important that this value system be conformable to the pastor's total theology.

4. The church musician should be able to relate his or her musical expertise to the broader concept of Christian ministry.

Even as the pastor may tend to have a system of theology that excludes church music, the musician may have an understanding of the profession and disciplines of church music that excludes theology. In American theological education (outside of the liturgical denominations) there has been a regrettable history of a two-track system: the pastor takes one track, the church musician the other. Just as the minister's track tends to minimize musical involvement, that of the musician frequently has little time for theology and the nonmusical skills of ministry. As a result both musician and theologian have tended to be separated, each entrenched within his or her particular area of professional skill.

In addition, the musician is heir to another characteristic problem. Professional musical education has within it the dynamic that calls for remarkable submission to disciplines of skill development. Long, intense hours spent in practice and rehearsal become a life-style where the goal is musical perfection itself. This kind of discipline is imperative if one is to become a competent musician. But when this musician moves into the church this question must be faced: "How is the achieving of musical perfection related to the mission of the church?" The question may appear to be simple. However, it carries a complex system of implications and qualifications that makes a quick and simplistic answer inadequate. It is most important that the church musician carefully consider related issues that are not particularly musical in nature. This is territory in which the musician and the theologian can meet for conversation if the musician is willing to enter it.

5. A pastor need not be skilled in music but should know issues affecting church music.

It is not imperative that the pastor be able to sight-read music or direct a choir or know how to choose choir music. It is important that he or she be able to cope with such a question as, "Why have a choir?" It is hoped that the answer could be more sophisticated and theological than, for instance, "It adds variety to the service" or "It prepares people for the sermon."

The pastor need not be an expert on acoustics, but it is useful to have some idea about what the acoustical environment will do to help or hinder preaching, organ music, choir singing, and congregational participation in worship. It is the pastor's responsibility to make sure that appropriate questions are asked and adequate answers supplied where music is concerned.

In both of these examples the pastor's role does not call for technical or musical expertise. It does call for an awareness of just where and how such expertise is needed. This awareness identifies the area within which decisions must be made and the process of evaluation carried on.

6. A church musician need not be skilled in theology but should attempt to bring "music as an art form" to the higher understanding of "music as the ministry of the gospel."

The church musician must be able to read music, direct a choir, and know how to choose choir music. These are all musical skills appropriate to expect of one in this profession. However, the musician is inadequate as a church leader unless he or she also is willing to grapple with the question, "Why have a choir?" in terms of ministry. The highest concern of the professional church musician must be to identify and participate in the mission of the church. "Mission" is not a musical concept; it is a Biblical/theological one.

The issues that follow are all related to the above six statements. They are dealt with in a manner that assumes the basic importance of each of these principles.

Two

THE MUSIC
OF THE CONGREGATION

Music in the New Testament

In the New Testament the emphasis on music is upon personal or congregational singing. We find mention of the hymn sung by Jesus and his disciples at the end of the meal in the upper room (Matt. 26:30; Mark 14:26). Paul advises two of the young churches to "teach and admonish one another in all wisdom, and . . . sing psalms and hymns and spiritual songs with thankfulness in your hearts to God" (Col. 3:16; cf. Eph. 5:19). He suggests to the Corinthian church that "I will sing with the spirit and I will sing with the mind also" (I Cor. 14:15). James exhorts any of his readers who are suffering to pray; any who are cheerful to sing praise (James 5:13). Paul and Silas exemplify the same convictions in the Philippian jail as they first pray and then sing (Acts 16:25). In Hebrews we find the affirmation, "In the midst of the congregation I will [sing] praise [to] thee" (Heb. 2:12), and similarly in Romans, "Therefore I will praise thee among the Gentiles, and sing to thy name" (Rom. 15:9). In Revelation we find singing a characteristic expression of the re-

deemed (Rev. 5:9; 14:3; 15:3), and in Luke the angels
sing (say?) their message of peace and goodwill (Luke
2:14). This comprises all the references to music in the
New Testament. There is no mention of musical instruments. There is no priestly system of instrumental musicians and choirs such as that of Solomon's Temple.

Historically some branches of the church have used
the limited nature of these musical references to construct a theology forbidding the use of instruments
and/or choirs. More commonly, such passages of Scripture have served to affirm priorities rather than to suggest restrictions. Without question, the New Testament
gives priority to the ordinary song of the believer. In
recognition of this, consideration of music in the church
should begin with congregational song. If this approach
is taken seriously, it means that the *primary* objective of
church musicians should be to implement and
strengthen the singing of all the people. There can be no
greater achievement in church music than encouraging,
teaching, and freeing the People of God to "sing praise
in the midst of the congregation."

This Biblical/theological priority will affect our view
of the role of the choir and our use of the organ. It will
be also an inescapable consideration as we build an
acoustical environment for the worship of the congregation. These matters will be considered specifically in the
appropriate chapters.

A HIERARCHY OF VALUES

Unfortunately, the vitality and the purposefulness that
characterize the New Testament references to singing
seem a bit at odds with the reality which many of us

experience from Sunday to Sunday. We may find the act of singing in worship to be an exciting one; on the other hand, it may be quite dull and dreary. Erik Routley suggests in *Hymns and Human Life:*

> The glory of our hymnody is in its power for converting unbelief, strengthening faith, and binding together the Christian community in that disciplined charity of which singing together is the symbol. The shame of our hymnody is in unreality, complacency, and spiritual slovenliness.[1]

A catalog of varied responses to congregational singing, arranged in a hierarchy from "best" to "worst," might be expressed in this fashion:

A. Highly meaningful, both cognitively and emotionally; able to affect understanding and valuing; might be described as "a moving experience"; a memorable occasion.

B. A pleasant experience, capable of reinforcing understandings and values; a welcome part of the total worship or fellowship experience.

C. A mechanical, thoughtless experience in which one participates with only partial involvement; no great loss if omitted; its value, if any, lies in other than musical or spiritual areas (e.g., to signal the beginning of a meeting or to give opportunity to stand and stretch).

D. A dull, perhaps boring experience without important purpose or meaning; the time spent would be better given to something more worthwhile.

E. An unpleasant or offensive experience; one in which the participants are uncomfortable, hoping it will soon be over.

Some comments about this hierarchy are the following:

1. It is reasonable to assume that the Biblical references to singing are best described by categories A and B.
2. Categories A and B are probably rare and unusual experiences.
3. Within any specific situation different persons may be experiencing the same occasion of singing at different levels.
4. A great deal of congregational singing takes place at level C or lower.
5. The simple hope or intention of the worship leader for singing to be at the higher levels is not enough to reach such an experience. Neither can this be done by admonishing the congregation to sing in such a fashion.

There are two ways of responding constructively to the desire for good singing. One is to identify dysfunctional factors that hinder the process and attempt to change them. The other is to consider factors that will implement a desirable experience. We will examine both.

DYSFUNCTIONAL ELEMENTS

Misuse

Within common church practice the high concept of Christian singing as expressed in the New Testament is frequently perverted to something utilitarian and mechanistic. The incongruity becomes apparent if one visualizes that scene in the upper room with Jesus and the disciples. If the occasion was the celebration of the Passover, that hymn which was sung at the end, by tradition, would have been the conclusion of the Hallel (Ps. 113 to 118). The singing of it would have been loaded with meaning and importance and memories. Can you conceive of Peter voicing such an invitation as: "Gentlemen, we've been sitting a long time. Let's stand and stretch and sing a hymn"?

To put it this way shifts the emphasis from singing as something important and meaningful in itself to the satisfying of some mundane physical or logistical need. Yet today's church frequently uses singing to provide opportunity to stand and stretch, to occupy the time until latecomers arrive, to give ushers opportunity to open or close the windows, to clear the tables after a meal, to give the choir or children a chance to move from one place to another, etc. None of these things is bad or wrong; most of them may be necessary. The thing that is unfortunate is the customary combining of them with the act of singing.

It is important to recognize the subtle way in which the constant use of congregational singing in such a manner may undermine the expectations of the worshipers. Such functional reasons, articulated by the leader and acted upon by the congregation, may be sharply contradictory to the actual content of that which is sung. The problem is not that some kind of profanity has taken place and a hymn denied proper respect. Rather, it is that by misuse the proper, higher function has been obscured. A chisel can be used as a screwdriver and may work perfectly well. However, if it continues to be used in this way, its capacity to perform its original intended function is destroyed. Even so with singing.

Another similar problem can be identified. It is a com-

mon practice to use singing as a means of getting ready
to do something else. Thus singing becomes a kind of
"preparation." For example, a "prayer song" becomes
not a prayer itself but rather something to quiet the room
and get persons ready to pray. In such a case the music
may help the experience of the spoken or silent prayer
that follows. But this practice will also tend to erode
meaningful (New Testament) singing, simply because it
is perceived as a tool to accomplish a related task rather
than being something of importance in itself.

The way we unconsciously speak about singing may
reveal how we truly perceive it. I have been in many
worship services as a visiting preacher where the pastor
was guiding the service as worship leader. Frequently I
choose a hymn whose words are a prayer and invite the
congregation to make the singing of the hymn the beginning of the morning prayer, which will then continue on
as the pastor leads in spoken prayer. This will be discussed before the service with the pastor and explained,
at the time, to the congregation. In spite of this, more
often than not, the pastor will step to the pulpit after the
hymn and say instinctively, "Let us pray." This reflects
a deeply ingrained habit of failing to recognize the possibility of "real" prayer as being anything but the spoken
word. To put it another way, this represents the inability
to think of congregational singing as anything but pre-
liminary to something else.

Again, the unconscious orientation of the pastor will
be revealed in the statement, *"Before* we begin, let's sing
a hymn," or "Let's sing a hymn, after which Deacon——
will open the meeting with prayer." Or, consider the
situation in which the leader invites the congregation to
sing "to let the people outside know that it's time to

begin." Predictably, the content of such "opening hymns" will be exuberant expressions of praise and affirmation. The New Testament speaks of such singing, but never in the context of expediting the logistics of the situation.

Such habitual diverting of congregational song to serve utilitarian purposes inevitably leads to a response characterized by meaninglessness.

Meaninglessness

Whenever the obvious sensible thrust of a hymn text is ignored and singing serves another unrelated task, the participant is faced with a choice. Does one attempt to respond honestly, creatively, and personally to the ideas being sung, and disregard the songleader's attention upon his or her watch and exhortations for those within hearing to "come on in"? In some cases the answer is "Yes." It is possible that such extraneous factors can be transcended. However, it is more likely that the participant will simply accept the announced agenda (for example, "getting the people in") and pay little attention to the words of the hymn. In such a situation one no longer seeks for meaning and involvement in that which is being sung. Instead, the mind and will withdraw to other areas while the singing continues. Syllables and musical notes follow one another unnoticed, each drawing the other along in familiar relationship. No attention need be given; the situation has disintegrated. Singing has become meaningless.

Another factor that reduces the level of meaning is lack of "readiness." It is a common but mistaken assumption that simply because Christians have gathered in a

particular place at a particular time, they are thereby
instantly ready to sing any kind of song, and sing it well.
It is the function of the music and the poetic imagery to
have emotional implications. A song may be highly personal. It may call for dramatic expression of praise or
love or contrition—expressions that may not reflect at all
the consciousness of the moment. In such a situation, the
worshiper's response may well be that of participating in
the appropriate act (making musical sounds) without actually engaging in the essential meaning of that act. It is
true that environment does tend to generate a certain
degree of readiness, but it is unrealistic to expect this
environment to consistently and immediately motivate
good singing.

One result of habitually engaging in meaningless experiences is the development of apathy.

Apathy

When congregational singing becomes meaningless
through misuse, motivation for excited and significant
participation is reduced or destroyed. The worshiper
easily drops into the habit of marginal, partial engagement. Church leaders often lament that members of the
congregation come to worship with an apathetic attitude.
Yet these leaders fail to recognize the variety of practices
that have worked across a long period of time to create
such passivity.

Musically related factors may contribute to an apathetic response. It is characteristic of the church's regular
worship that its liturgy, formal or informal, includes elements that are continually repeated. In congregational
music, this may be particular songs that are frequently

sung; it may be simply a regular predictable pattern of singing within the service. Such things have both a positive and a negative function. Positively, they serve to provide a familiar climate that can be reassuring and reinforcing. Persons need this element in their lives, and its presence is not necessarily contradictory to the objectives of the church. Negatively, such things are constantly in danger of becoming invisible, unnoticed. Speaking of this in *Thomas Wingate, Curate,* George Macdonald said, "Nothing is so deadening to the divine as an habitual dealing with the outsides of holy things."[2] An experienced churchgoer easily develops the ability to set the mouth going on the friendly pathway of a familiar hymn while the mind is busy elsewhere. This phenomenon usually accompanies other problems which have been discussed above. When that is the case a simple exhortation to "give attention to what you are singing; sing with meaning!" will probably not change anything. It may, itself, become part of the familiar unnoticed pattern.

Apathy may also refer to something beyond the too-familiar act of singing; it may describe a person's (congregation's) response to the total act of worship—even to the whole of the Christian faith. If there is no meaningful engagement with the living Christ, no involvement in a gospel that provides purpose and gives meaning to life, then it is too much to expect that singing will of itself bring vitality (although this can happen). The New Testament comments about music were made in the context of living out a dynamic life of faith.

The three problems identified as misuse, meaninglessness, and apathy have been presented above in overdrawn manner—something of a caricature. Some of these dysfunctional elements may be present and yet worthwhile singing still may happen. The point is simply this: When these practices become the regular, predictable approach to congregational music, the whole service will inevitably suffer. When the pastor or church musician forms the habit of using singing in these dysfunctional ways, then the likelihood of experiencing music as the New Testament suggests is diminished or lost.

SUCCESSFUL ELEMENTS

A positive approach to this area of ministry could reasonably begin with a simple call to awareness—recognition of the dangers inherent in the dysfunctional aspects and a desire to avoid them. Alternatives to misuse, meaninglessness, and apathy are available.

To quote Erik Routley again: he has suggested that a good hymn is one that has been "well written, well chosen, and well sung."[3] This statement could also serve to characterize good congregational singing.

Well-Written Hymn

The first aspect of the hymn to be examined should be its theology. Any hymn used by the church should be theologically sound. A song should not be chosen that contradicts the doctrinal position of the church, either by forceful explicit statement or by overall emphasis. No hymn should ever be used simply because it has a pleasant tune. Rather, the user should be able to affirm in general its basic theological thrust.

A great deal of theology is firmly established in the consciousness and affections of a congregation through the hymns it comes to know and love. A contemporary novelist has expressed this in a conversation about the church organist and "one of the hymns he used to play, and you and I used to sing before we grew up and got elegant. That's a lovely thing about hymns: we never forget them, do we? Like limericks, God knew a thing or two when He invented rhyme."[4]

Karl Barth, in an aside in his *Church Dogmatics*, reminisced concerning the songs he learned as a child:

> This [the hymn book] was the text-book in which, at the beginning of the last decade of the last century, I received my first theological instruction in a form appropriate to my then immaturity. And what made an indelible impression on me was the homely naturalness with which these very modest compositions spoke of the events of Christmas, Palm Sunday, Good Friday, Easter, the Ascension and Pentecost as things which might take place any day in Basel or its environs like any other important happenings. History? Doctrine? Dogma? Myth? No—but things actually taking place, so that we could see and hear and lay up in our hearts. For as these songs were sung in the everyday language we were then beginning to hear and speak, and as we joined in singing, we took our mother's hand, as it were, and went to the stall at Bethlehem, and to the streets of Jerusalem where, greeted by children of a similar age, the Saviour made His entry, and to the dark hill of Golgotha, and as the sun rose to the garden of Joseph. . . . Yes, it was very naive, but perhaps in the very naivety there lay the deepest wisdom and greatest power, so that once grasped it was calculated to carry one relatively unscathed—although not, of course, untempted or unassailed—through all the serried ranks of historicism and anti-historicism, mysticism and rationalism, orthodoxy, liberalism and existentialism, and to bring one back some day to the matter itself.[5]

It is imperative that these songs which affect persons so powerfully should contain the truth concerning the gospel.

However, this criterion must be used with reasonable flexibility, not with rigid dogmatism. Poetic expression will not always have either the precision or the comprehensiveness of a creedal statement. Many good hymns could be faulted because they present only one aspect of a particular doctrine. The responsibility for singing the full counsel of God belongs not to the hymn writer but to the one who chooses the songs and who creates the contexts in which they are sung.

All of the above is an argument for taking seriously the timeless, universal hymns of the church. Those which have persisted through the sifting process of a century or more tend to deal with the widely accepted affirmations of Christian faith. For example, during their years of contemporaneous ministry, Charles Wesley and Augustus Toplady fought bitterly over their differing theological positions (Arminian vs. Calvinist). Today their respective hymns ("Jesus, Lover of My Soul" and "Rock of Ages") are found as close neighbors in most hymnals. And who, even in the most conservative or orthodox churches, is concerned that "In the Cross of Christ I Glory" and "It Came Upon the Midnight Clear" were written by Unitarians (Sir John Bowring and Edmund Sears)? The only thing that matters is that these hymns are compatible with the theological understanding and constructs of many churches.

We have been considering theological soundness. What about theological usefulness? Two illustrations can identify the issue.

There are many traditional hymns whose imagery is

rooted in the concept of the "holy war." No matter that some of these are favorite songs or that this imagery is based upon Scripture. Today, for some thoughtful Christians, this imagery has become inappropriate. Many who have experienced the trauma of Vietnam and of the religious wars in Ireland and the Near East find it difficult to sing about the church's mission in these terms. "Sound the Battle Cry," "The Son of God Goes Forth to War," "Onward, Christian Soldiers," "Am I a Soldier of the Cross?" "Soldiers of Christ, Arise," "Stand Up, for Jesus, Ye Soldiers of the Cross," and other similar expressions are incompatible in today's world with the sharing of the good news about the love of God as seen in Jesus Christ. The fact that many of us in the church do not connect such songs with the reality reported in the daily newspaper strongly points up the issue. Though we may simply enjoy the tunes and the vigorous cadence and ignore the words, they speak explicitly to those outside the fellowship—those with whom we want to share the gospel. They are not theologically useful.

Similarly, at this moment in our society the issue of sexism is becoming important to many. Emotional debate is going on as to whether all exclusive sexist language should or can be eliminated from the hymnbook. At such a time, if such persons are part of the worshiping community, it is questionable whether a hymn with the focus of "Rise Up, O Men of God" or "Men and Children Everywhere" can be considered useful.

The consideration of specific technical matters that might identify a hymn text or tune as being "well written" is beyond the scope of this book. Such matters are dealt with extensively in Austin Lovelace's *The Anatomy of Hymnody,* Erik Routley's two books *Hymns Today and To-*

morrow and *The Music of Christian Hymnody,* and in a delightful article by Gracia Grindal, "Language, A Lost Craft Among Hymn Writers."[6]

However, more guidance is easily available. In the case of historical hymns the process of selection by the church offers some help. This goes beyond theological matters to include the use of language and music.

In the eighteenth century Charles Wesley wrote approximately 6,500 hymn texts. Only 253 of these are still included in the major English-language hymnals of the twentieth century.[7] Thus, for example, one of the favorite hymns of the late eighteenth and early nineteenth centuries was his "Ah! Lovely Appearance of Death":

> Ah! Lovely appearance of death!
> What sight upon earth is so fair:
> Not all the gay pageants that breathe
> Can with a dead body compare.
> With solemn delight I survey
> The corpse, when the Spirit has fled,
> In love with the beautiful clay,
> And longing to lie in its stead.

Even though it was sung at the memorial service for George Whitefield in Philadelphia in 1770, it no longer appears in any major hymnal. But other hymns of Wesley persist. For more than two centuries, generations of Christians in many differing cultures and denominations have continued to affirm the remarkable quality and value of his "O for a Thousand Tongues to Sing," "Hark! the Herald Angels Sing," and "Christ the Lord Is Risen Today." As with great works of art, the persistent, continuing existence of these hymns is their own validation. "What the Church universal adopts and cherishes is, by that fact, removed from the control of a picking pedantry and of a cold-blooded correctness."[8] Any text in the hymnbook which was written more than one hundred and fifty years ago is likely to be well written.

The term "well written" obviously refers to the way theology, language, and music are used in the construction of a hymn. However, let us consider another aspect of the hymn which lies beyond or beneath the words and music as they appear on the pages of the hymnal. Many of these hymns have been the expression and possession of the church for many generations, even many centuries, persisting across cultural, geographical, and denominational lines. These timeless universal songs not only demonstrate a quality of craftsmanship but also represent the church's memory. They are the expressions of our Christian neighbors in space and time. Written by Christians across nineteen centuries of the church's life, they witness to faith by both Protestants and Catholics. Dietrich Bonhoeffer affirmed this as he wrote:

> It is the voice of the Church that is heard in singing together. It is not you that sings, it is the Church that is singing, and you, as a member of the Church, may share in its song. Thus all singing together that is right must serve to widen our Spiritual horizon, make us see our little company as a member of the great Christian Church on earth, and help us willingly and gladly to join our singing, be it feeble or good, to the song of the Church.[9]

These hymns have found their origins in a variety of denominations, and come from many countries. They contain a distillate of Christian faith and life, expressing the basic reality of the unity of the church as the one body of Christ. All of this, while true, may not be a part of the awareness of minister or congregation. They encounter the hymn simply as one among similar musical items in the hymnbook. Thus this remarkable and unique aspect of Christian hymnody is unrecognized by many Christians.

While part of the value and meaning of a hymn lies simply in what it says, another value lies in understanding who said it, why, and when. Also, awareness of when, where, and why the *singing* of a particular hymn has had special meaning for the Christian community can be of value. For example, the hymns of Paul Gerhardt from the Thirty Years' War of the seventeenth century provided strength and help for Dietrich Bonhoeffer during his imprisonment as a twentieth-century martyr.[10] The fact that Gerhardt's affirmations of faith came out of the context of an earlier war gave these hymns an added dimension of meaning for Bonhoeffer in his imprisonment for his faith during the Second World War.

Once this aspect of congregational music is recognized and desired, one can consult the many excellent books that deal with the historic life and faith experiences out of which our hymns have come.[11]

Well-Chosen Hymn

The process of choosing hymns involves response both to the immediate situation and also to the long-range needs of the congregation. Let us consider first these broad and basic long-range concerns.

Songs for congregational use exist in a great variety of styles and types. Reference was made above to timeless, persistent universal hymns. Examples of such hymns, originals and English translations, would be "O Sacred Head, Now Wounded" (twelfth, seventeenth, and nine-

teenth centuries), "A Mighty Fortress Is Our God" (six-
teenth and nineteenth centuries), "Our God, Our Help
in Ages Past" (eighteenth century). These represent one
distinctive body of Christian music. Over against these
ancient expressions is the enormous number of contemporary colloquial songs (which will be discussed in Chapter 8, "Age of Rock and Rock of Ages?"). Somewhere
between these two is the gospel song, which is the expression of late-nineteenth-century American evangelism. Each of these types has distinctive values; the
maturing and full Christian experience has need of all of
them. However, it is a common phenomenon that a particular congregation will attach itself to one or another
of these styles. Over a period of time that particular
music then comes to be the expression which identifies
and expresses a "proper" Christian experience.

To illustrate: many congregations sing only gospel
songs, viewing them as the "good old hymns." In reality,
this idiom is only about one hundred years old. It gained
its great popularity in England and America through its
use in the evangelistic meetings of Dwight L. Moody and
his musician, Ira Sankey. The music was similar to the
popular "parlor music" of the day. The texts tend to
focus on the experience of meeting Christ—of salvation.
They are cast in the first person, speaking of *my* sin, *my*
coming to the cross, *my* continuing walk with Jesus.

None of this is bad. The church needs this kind of
experience and expression. As a responsible American
musicologist has said:

> Gospel hymnody has the distinction of being America's
> most typical contribution to Christian song. Gospel hym-
> nody has been a plough digging up the hardened surfaces

of pavemented minds. Its very obviousness has been its strength. Where delicacy or dignity can make no impress, gospel hymnody stands up triumphing. Sankey's songs are true folk music of the people.[12]

The problem lies in the practice of singing *only* gospel songs. Sankey would never have understood such a practice. These songs were meant only for evangelistic meetings—not for the ongoing life and worship of the church. He expected that churches would continue to use traditional hymns. His first American hymnal, *Gospel Hymns and Sacred Songs,* was published in 1875 for the gospel meetings. The first song in this book is "Old Hundredth" —"All People That on Earth Do Dwell," a sixteenth-century metrical psalm. Almost one third of the songs in that first book of gospel songs are from earlier generations. They truly represent the timeless, universal expression of worship. However, in the century since Sankey, many congregations have avoided these earlier hymns and limited their singing to the personal songs of salvation. Such a practice, with its restricted possibilities of Christian expression and experience is unfortunate in terms of limiting Christian maturation.

Fortunately many such congregations are discovering a deeper and broader singing experience. Editors of many contemporary hymnals are encouraging such expansion. For example, the *Broadman Hymnal* of 1940, familiar to many Southern Baptists and other free-church congregations, had about 62 percent gospel songs; in contrast, the *New Broadman Hymnal* of 1977 has about 29 percent. The 33 percent which represents the difference between the two is made up of more ancient/traditional hymns and of a number of truly contemporary songs.

A second general matter relating to the choosing of hymns has to do with the previous comment about the dangers inherent in usually choosing hymns to *prepare* for something. "Choosing well" may invite the reversal of the process. Instead of thinking of singing as a preparation, one might consider its highest potential function as the congregation's *response* to something that has occurred—the expression of a preexisting readiness. Thus a song might be the appropriate congregational reaction to a particular passage of Scripture, to an event occurring within the time of worship, or to some occurrence within the larger experience of the community (for example, a tragic or remarkably fortunate event—which would, of course, need to be identified to give the meaning to the subsequent song). A time of prayer, an anthem by the choir, or a particular point in the sermon could provide the stimulus to which the hymn was the response. If the song grows obviously and immediately out of another experience, there will be no need to exhort the congregation to sing "with spirit and with understanding." This relating of song to readiness may be either a spontaneous reaction or the result of careful planning.

After consideration is given to these general matters, then a number of specifics will affect a particular choice. What particular idea is desired? In what mood should this idea be expressed? This relates to the musical setting. For example, "Lead On, O King Eternal" and "Where He Leads Me I Will Follow" are similar ideologically, but obviously they are quite different in terms of mood. What about familiarity? If a song is strange to the congregation, they will probably not find any great meaning in struggling with it. Generally, new tunes must be taught in a self-conscious learning experience before they can be usefully sung. If readiness is minimal, the song should be familiar and without musical difficulties. Potential difficulties include such things as a high beginning note or tessitura ("Now Thank We All Our God"), lack of momentum ("Be Still, My Soul"), awkward intervals ("My Jesus, as Thou Wilt"), unusual rhythmic or metrical patterns ("He Who Would Valiant Be"). If readiness is high, then these matters of musical difficulty are of lesser or no importance.

A comment concerning the selection of stanzas is appropriate here. There is no reason to feel that all stanzas of a hymn need always be sung—that we must somehow preserve the author's intended statement intact. In many cases this is impossible. Isaac Watts's "Our God, Our Help in Ages Past" was originally written in nine stanzas; his "When I Survey the Wondrous Cross" in five. Charles Wesley's "Hark! the Herald Angels Sing" and his "O for a Thousand Tongues to Sing" both had ten stanzas. No contemporary hymnal prints all of these. "Jesus, the Very Thought of Thee" is part of an original Latin poem of forty-eight lines, and "Jesus, Thou Joy of Loving Hearts" is simply a different translation of some lines from the same original. Thus, in many cases, the original hymn has been changed by deletion of stanzas, editorial alterations, and translator's license before we ever encounter it. A blind legalistic commitment to the total hymn as it happens to be printed in the book is unrealistic.

Stanzas may properly be omitted if the hymn is too long for the occasion, if they deal with matters that seem irrelevant to the moment of singing, or if part of the hymn uses language or expressions that are inappropriate for the group.

Concerning length, four or five stanzas of a text in Double Common Meter or 10s or 11s may easily be too long for a particular situation, especially if they are set to a tune that tends to move slowly. On the other hand, concerning sheer length, it is rarely wise to use just one stanza. This will present no problem when the singing is from memory. However, psychologically, the time of singing needs to be longer than the time spent on the logistics of finding a page, waiting for an introduction to be played, and, perhaps, standing to sing.

Concerning the ideological content, there may or may not be a need to hold certain stanzas together. "God of Grace and God of Glory" has five long stanzas (8787877), each of which is complete in itself. It may be perfectly appropriate to choose from among these any that focus on the desired emphasis. "Come, Thou Almighty King" is a series of stanzas, each of which deals with one person of the Trinity. These are sequential but not interdependent. The inclusion or omission of any of them depends on whether the whole Trinitarian concept is desired or whether some other emphasis is central. "Nearer, My God, to Thee" is the telling in stanzas 2 to 4 of the story of Jacob at Bethel. To choose stanzas 1, 3, and 5—as is sometimes done with a five-stanza hymn— is to invite the singing of nonsense. Stanza 3 is meaningless except as it relates to Jacob's experience. (Unfortunately, the congregation seldom protests being invited to sing nonsense.) With "A Mighty Fortress Is Our God," stanzas 1 and 2 offer one complete idea, stanzas 3 and 4 another. To sing the first and last stanzas of this particular long hymn is, again, meaningless. The first stanza alone stands as a hymn of praise to Satan; the last begins in the midst of an idea. Many hymns such as "My Jesus,

I Love Thee" have a final stanza or two which shift the
focus from the basic idea of the hymn to something es-
chatological—usually death or heaven. This expression
is certainly relevant for the church but may not be appropriate to a particular occasion.

The third reason for "tailoring" a hymn has to do with
the use of language. One illustration may be the romantic
Victorian hymn or gospel song which is basically still
useful but which may contain a bit of strange, old-fash-
ioned expression. The first and third stanzas of "Blessed
Assurance, Jesus Is Mine!" still express a basically good
idea in words that are useful today. The second stanza,
however, speaks of "visions of rapture now burst on my
sight"; of "angels descending, bringing from above
Echoes of mercy, whispers of love." Like Wesley's "Ah!
Lovely Appearance of Death," these images may be
grounded in aspects of Christianity that are still important, but they are expressed in ways that are curiously
archaic today. It is possible to avoid some of these without discarding the song itself. Similarly exclusive, sexist
language is often used or focused only in a stanza or two
and can be easily avoided by the omitting of those stanzas.

As a general principle, one may use any or all of the
stanzas, choosing those which make sense and contain
the ideas and language appropriate for a particular occasion.

One of the thorniest questions relating to the choosing of hymns has to do, not with How? but with Who?
This becomes part of the still larger question of who is
to plan the worship service. Leaving that discussion for
later, I wish to suggest a few factors related to hymn
selection.

Some denominations are quite specific about this responsibility, leaving it clearly in the hands of the pastor. Others—for example, Baptists—may not specify such responsibility but by tradition and for pragmatic reasons it may gravitate toward the pastor. In any case, as far as the choosing of hymns is concerned, issues are involved that suggest that this should be a cooperative activity.

The pastor may or may not be sensitive to musical factors involved. At least, he or she will know a group of familiar hymns, categorized as opening hymns, prayer hymns, general hymns, invitation hymns. The pastor will probably attempt to use those of each category in rotation, and may keep a log in order to avoid the overuse of any one. He or she may approach the matter of hymn selection ideologically, attempting to connect each hymn with a particular idea or theme. This approach carries with it the danger of being insufficiently responsive to musical aspects of the hymn.

If the choice is left to the musician, it may, again, be made on the basis of favorites. However, the musician's favorites may well be different from those of the pastor. Many times the musician's training develops attitudes toward the church's hymnody which are based only on musical excellence—or the lack of it. The ability to discriminate in this way can be helpful in enriching a congregation's singing experience; it can also be the basis for intolerance.

The factors that affect the choosing of hymns are of many kinds. Some are theological, some functional, some musical, and some pastoral. These, in turn, are inextricably linked to others involved in bringing about good singing—the "well sung" aspect of the process. Because of this, the process of choosing should involve the particular expertise of both pastor and musician. Both will contribute in terms of their own taste and their perceptions of the need of congregation and choir. The pastor may be more sensitive ideologically or theologically and will best be able to think of hymns as response to Scripture, prayer, sermon which are chosen by him or her. The musician may have a better feel for matters of musical style and mood. He or she will be particularly sensitive to the issue of singability, and perhaps familiarity. The musician will know what hymn materials will require rehearsal by the choir and which ones might be enriched by the use of related organ and choral materials. The point is not to characterize the way the pastor's view of a hymn differs from the musician's. That is impossible; there is too much difference in individual interests and experiences. Nevertheless, it is likely that these two individuals will come to this issue with differing concerns. If there are differences of values, criteria, and objectives, the sharing and working out of these differences can be the occasion for creative exploration. It can also be the means of generating a richer worship experience than either could plan alone.

Well-Sung Hymn

Many elements can affect the success of congregational singing. The most important of these has to do with motivation or purposefulness, and in essence that has been the focus of this chapter. When people truly want to sing, are ready to sing, and have been given an appropriate song through which to express this readiness, then the effects of other matters are minimized. Nevertheless, other considerations might well be identified.

Focus

The problem previously labeled "misuse" might have been identified in part by the term "misdirection." The offense is not totally that something else takes place at the same time as singing. It is that a secondary function is talked about and put forth as the reason for singing. Another approach is possible. It recognizes or anticipates a logistical need, and then chooses a hymn or plans a time of singing of appropriate length. The difference lies in the attitude of the leader of the service, who will avoid such terminology as "While we are waiting . . . ." Expectations will be focused in the area of spiritual value rather than utilitarian function, and the advance consideration will reflect such an objective. The worship leader should realize that there is no real need always to attempt to conceal logistical functions behind a screen of congregational song.

Tempo

The most important consideration related to tempo is purely pragmatic. The tempo should be one at which the hymn *can* be sung well. Excessive slowness may result from congregational lethargy, lack of ability on the part of the accompanist, or an unrealistic striving for some mood such as "majesty or dignity." An excessively fast tempo is usually a reactionary attempt by accompanist or minister to combat the problem of slowness. The tempo is too slow (1) when breaths must be taken in the middle of words or phrases to carry them to conclusion, (2) when there is a sense of loss of momentum, which leads to (3) a feeling that the song is interminably long and drawn out. The tempo is too fast when it becomes difficult for the singers actually to form the syllables and notes. Organists, particularly, need to be sensitive to the easy possibility of their fingers moving faster than the congregation can possibly sing.

Acoustics

The subject of acoustics is considered in Chapter 7, "Acoustics and Worship." Good congregational singing is virtually impossible in an acoustical environment like that of a mortuary "slumber room," which functions to inhibit or stifle the making of any kind of sound.

Familiarity—The Too-familiar

As was the case with the issue of tempo, the problems here are opposite and equal. At one extremity are the songs that are too familiar; these run the risk of inviting meaningless or apathetic response. Anything that can be done to provide an aspect of newness can be helpful. This might involve changing the manner or the place of use—for example, as part of the pastoral prayer or within the context of the sermon where appropriate. Even such a simple thing as having the congregation remain seated while singing at a point where they are accustomed to standing can subtly improve the level of their response. A feeling of newness may be encouraged by altering the familiar musical setting. This can be done by making new combinations of familiar texts and tunes.[13] It can also be the result of the use of "free" accompaniment by organ or piano on occasional stanzas.

Familiarity—The Unfamiliar

The problem of the unfamiliar hymn is obvious though not always conceded. Not all worshipers are capable of sight-reading a new hymn. Many of those who can are unwilling to make the effort. The answer to this situation lies in advance preparation. When a totally new hymn is to be used, the choir, at least, must have become familiar and comfortable with it. Perhaps the organist will have played the tune several times as part of prelude, offertory, or postlude on previous occasions. Possibly other members of the congregation (for example, members of children's or youth choirs or of particular church school classes) will have had some encounter with and rehearsal of it. Finally, a brief congregational rehearsal immediately before the service in which it is being used should be considered.

It is well to assume that usually no new hymn will be enjoyed as much as a familiar one. This will be especially true if the congregation is used to singing mainly gospel songs and traditional or contemporary choruses. Characteristically these are essentially simplistic and easy to sing. That is their unique value. They provide a kind of music and text that is easy to learn and remember.

In contrast to these, traditional hymnody will feel stiff, formal, and difficult. No matter that the imagery may be richer and more provocative. No matter that the tune may have a feeling of weight and timelessness ("Ein' feste Burg" or "Lobe den Herren"). No matter that it may offer a richer though more complex sense of variety and purposefulness ("Lasst uns erfreuen," "Aberystwyth," "Mit Freuden zart"). Probably it will not be very rewarding the first time it is attempted.

The answer, then, is to attempt to teach a congregation only a few new hymns of this type in the course of a year; to teach these few very well; and to choose them with great care, since so much importance is to be given such a small number of them. Many churches try a "hymn of the month" program at some time and usually discover its value to be mainly academic. Exposure to something new is not the same as learning or valuing something new. To put it simply, a new hymn has not been taught until the congregation has learned it. A congregation that knows and loves "He Lives" may be exposed to "Jesus Lives and So Shall I" for a few weeks, but the congregation's affections will probably remain with the former. The fact that the latter is one of the rich, timeless, universal expressions of the church is not enough to shift affection to it. It takes more than a few weeks for such a hymn to be learned well enough to be sung easily. More than that, hymns are not loved and enjoyed simply because of the nature of their text and tune. There are associations with ideas and experiences which have accompanied the act of singing a particular hymn. It takes many months to develop both familiarity and associational values. Most congregations can accomplish the learning of only three or four such hymns at this deep level in the course of a year.

In such a teaching process, the hymn should be introduced with help from the organ, the choir, other groups, and with congregational rehearsal. Then it should be sung as often and as widely within the church as possible —several times a week, both in worship and in other meetings, and in the choirs' rehearsals. The choir members should memorize all the stanzas. This should continue for several weeks until people are beginning to tire of it. It is only at that point that they have really begun to learn the song. *After* it has been learned is the time when the pastor or the musician should attempt to make ideological or experiential connectives. *Then* it can be used as the appropriate congregational response to a particular sermon or passage of Scripture. To attempt this at the time of its introduction ignores the fact that a congregation preoccupied with the struggle of singing a new and difficult hymn is unable to give very much concern to its meaning.

Finally, after the hymn has been learned and has acquired some particular meaning, it should be repeated every few weeks. Then it will have become part of the familiar hymnological vocabulary of the congregation. At that point it is probably better to put this learning process aside for a few weeks before starting on another hymn with similar intensity. During this learning period, care should be taken to see that the other hymns included in the service will be comfortable, familiar ones.

Obviously, the process described above is not necessary or appropriate for the learning of a simple chorus that can be grasped and enjoyed at first encounter. Both kinds of learning should be part of the experience of any church.

As a congregation has successful experiences in learning new songs, both hymns and choruses, a kind of readiness to learn will begin to develop. A sense of achievement leads to heightened motivation for other new ventures. A congregation that has such experiences is on its way to becoming one that is open to new experiences —one that welcomes them.

Accompaniment

Most congregations and many choirs receive their primary stimulus and guidance in singing from the piano or organ rather than from some other leader (whether or not there is such other leader). Because of this it is of greatest importance that the instrumental leadership be confident and competent. This requirement seems unrealistic for the church that does not seem to have a proficient musician available. However, such a situation should suggest two things. First, it should encourage a sense of urgency to the problem of finding an instrumentalist of adequate competence. The level of congregational singing is unlikely to transcend the skill of the accompanist. Second, it should illuminate the need for serious and intensive rehearsal of the hymn on the part of a mediocre musician. (This in turn will require the selection of these hymns well in advance on the part of the minister and the musician.)

Leadership

It should be apparent by now that the factors involved in good congregational singing are not all musical. When a context for choosing appropriate hymns has been fully explored, a great deal of the task of leadership has been accomplished. There are additional matters that lie in the province of music itself—matters such as questions of key relationships, comparative musical difficulty of tunes, comparative emotional characteristics of tunes, the physical conducting of the music (when necessary and appropriate).

The situation divides itself this way: Things that have

to do with readiness and appropriateness relate strongly to the *texts* of hymns. No musical training or skill is necessary to work with these words; any minister or church school leader already has the necessary capability. Things that have to do with the *tunes* require the involvement of a musician. The implications of this dichotomy are these: First, when musical expertise is not available, the possibility of using hymn texts as poetry without feeling compelled to try to sing them should be taken seriously. This has been a common practice of Christians for centuries. In fact, a great many hymns were originally written as poems rather than as song texts. Second, that an important part of the singing experience grows out of the nature of the tunes themselves should be recognized. While texts can be used without concern for music, if music is to be involved, then some musical awareness is needed in order that appropriate judgments can be made. Third, this should suggest a desirable relationship of pastor and church musician wherein each can share expertise and objectives with the other as both work together to achieve the common goal of ministry.

Three

THE CHOIR

This chapter will not deal with procedures and materials to be used in the training of church choirs. Many good books are available for that! Rather, it seeks to present some issues that have to do with the meaning and style of the choir's existence, with a few related functional examples. It is quite possible that questions raised here might be answered one way by the pastor and another by the choir director. If so, the very nature of Christian ministry would suggest the appropriateness of discussion between them with a hope of achieving better understanding which might lead to change and growth on the part of both individuals.

WHY HAVE A CHOIR?

"And when the song was raised [by singers, with trumpets and cymbals], . . . the house of the LORD was filled with a cloud, so that the priests could not stand to minister because of the cloud; for the glory of the LORD filled the house of God." (II Chron. 5:13–14.)

This is an excellent passage of Scripture to invoke at

a choir banquet or a choir recognition service. It describes the singing of the Levitical choir with its 288 singers (I Chron., ch. 25) and 4,000 musicians in all (I Chron., ch. 23). They were led by Asaph, Heman, and Jeduthun, and accompanied by cymbals, harps, lyres, and 120 trumpeters. As they sang, the glory of the Lord was revealed through the music with such power that all other ministry had to stop for a time. What could be more fulfilling for a choir member or a director!

This is one of the few detailed Biblical accounts of the functioning of the choir in worship. As was mentioned earlier, there is no comment concerning the existence of choirs in the New Testament (except, perhaps, the poetic description in Rev., ch. 14, of the new song which is sung by the 144,000). The Levitical priests, which included the temple musicians, have now been replaced by the priesthood of all believers. The concept of an elaborate system of worship has been superseded by worship "in spirit and truth" which no longer finds its focus in either the Jerusalem or the Samaritan temple (John 4:19ff.). What place does this leave for the choir?

Throughout much of the life of the Christian church it has been assumed that this priestly function should continue. Thus, many of the medieval cathedrals located the choir near the altar, behind a screen or within an enclosure, where the monks and clergy as singers sat facing each other and made their musical offering to God. The laity did not participate. In fact, they frequently could not even see what was happening. They could only overhear and be vicariously involved.

In a much more recent American tradition, that of nineteenth-century mass evangelism, the role of the choir was the same as that of the evangelist. The task of the singers was to testify to their faith through music and to invite, even attempt to persuade, response on the part of the audience.

These two quite different traditions have affected church architecture where the placing of the choir is involved. The one has led to the arrangement of a divided chancel where the choir worships as did the medieval monks. The other has located the choir behind the central pulpit facing the congregation and addressing itself to them.

A third option, common in the eighteenth and nineteenth centuries in England and America in a wide variety of churches, gathered singers and instrumentalists in a rear gallery. While their primary function was to assist the congregational singing, on occasion they offered special musical selections. At such time, in some situations, it was the practice for the congregation to stand, turn around, and "face the music." (The present meaning of this phrase provides a commentary on the competence of some of these little bands of musicians.)[14] In recent years, a modern version of this concept has appeared wherein the choir is located with the congregation and perceived as part of it. Various attempts have been made to symbolize this idea architecturally. These are often within an overall concept of church-in-the-round, where the choir is seated so as to demonstrate its identification with the congregation rather than a separation from it.

This consideration of choir location is rooted in the issues of identity and function. The relevant question is, Why have a choir? or, perhaps, What is a choir supposed to do? There is no one generally accepted understanding of this. Each of the first two options mentioned above is affirmed by some churches. The third concept can be

illustrated by the discussion concerning worship found in
Kierkegaard's *Purify Your Hearts* of a century ago. There
he suggests that worship is not the minister and choir
speaking to God on behalf of the congregation; neither
is it exactly the reverse wherein the worship leaders attempt to speak for God to the congregation whose members are present as hearers. Rather, true worship, he
says, is that which goes on between each person in that
assembly and God. Thus the proper role of minister and
choir is to serve as "prompters," to use an analogy from
the stage. As Kierkegaard put it:

> The presence of God is the decisive fact that alters every-
> thing. Whenever God is present, it is everybody's business
> to take heed to himself before God, the preacher's [choir's]
> business to take heed to himself in his preaching, what he is
> to say, the hearer's business to take heed to himself when he
> is spoken to, how he attends and whether himself he is
> speaking secretly to God through the word that is
> preached.[15]

In such a situation there are no spectators, no priests
in the Levitical sense, and no performers (except to use
the term in Kierkegaard's analogy wherein every person
present is an "actor" and God is the Audience). Within
this concept the choir exists to prompt and enable each
worshiper to worship; each choir member is at the same
time prompter and individual worshiper before God.

The critical issue here is not that we must be able to
establish which one of these understandings about the
choir in worship is universally right, good, and true.
Rather, it is that we should recognize the variety of concepts and attempt to decide which is closest to our own
position. Having done this, we need further to recognize

the implications which develop from that particular position.

Let me give an example of a specific functional question whose answer might be affected by the way this theological issue is understood. Frequently, churches are troubled as to precisely what kind of persons should be members of the choir. Should membership be limited to church members? to any persons who are able clearly to identify themselves as Christians? to all persons who like to sing and have an interest in the project? to a select and competent group of hired professionals? An important element (though not the only one) in resolving this question will be a clear understanding of the choir's role.

If the choir exists to carry on a priestly function, then all of those who participate should be uniquely sanctified, set apart, as in the Levitical tradition. If this principle were logically adhered to, then the architect, contractor, and custodian might also need to be sanctified as were those from the original tribe of Levi who were charged with the building and care of the Temple.

If, like the evangelist or minister, the choir is understood as being engaged in witnessing to the congregation concerning their faith, then it is a reasonable expectation that choir members should be men and women of faith. However, if the choir is perceived as being one with the congregation, engaged in offering music as a stimulus for worship, then the restrictions upon its membership should reasonably be neither more nor less than the restrictions appropriate for any member of the congregation.

Curious and inconsistent things happen when the choir's role is viewed at times as that of priest, at other times as evangelist, and still others as enabler. To respond, "I favor a bit of each," is to fail to take seriously the substantial differences that exist between these concepts. My own commitment is to a view of the choir as enabler. Within this concept, it is appropriate and desirable that, like members in the congregation, choir members should be continually taking steps of Christian growth (committing themselves to Christ, seeking membership in his church, etc.). The remaining comments in this chapter are from the perspective of the choir as enabler.

The Choir and Congregational Music

Bringing together the New Testament emphasis upon congregational song and the concept of identifying the choir's role as prompter leads obviously to the absolute priority of the choir's responsibility toward congregational singing. We examine, then, some of the ways that this works out in practice.

First, when the choir sings by itself, it should be doing something that the congregation is not able to do. It is inappropriate if, in fact, the choir "anthem" turns out to be simply taking one of the congregational hymns for itself. In such a case, the congregation is better served by being allowed to do its own singing. This is not to suggest that hymn-related materials should never be used by the choir. To the contrary, they should comprise an important part of the repertoire of any church choir. However, what the choir brings to the service as special music should be something beyond the present capabilities of the congregation. This might mean, for the choir, to use a hymn from the church's hymnbook that is not known, perhaps one that might be a bit difficult for easy immediate use by all. It might mean singing a hymn, perhaps new or very old from another tradition, which is not in the hymnal. It could involve using a hymn text in a musical setting other than the familiar one in the present hymnbook—a setting that might invite fresh attention to an overly familiar text or that might suggest a new level of meaning. An example of this might be the recombining of text and a different tune to provide freshness and possibly to suggest a new association of ideas.[16] None of this is musically difficult, nor does it assume that the choir should seek a musically difficult task as something to be valued in itself. A meaningful hymn, sung simply and carefully in unison, can be a valuable contribution to worship by the choir.

There is an even more basic ministry related to congregational song. It lies within the power of even a small and unskilled choir to make congregational singing come alive. This involves rehearsal of a particular hymn until the choir is able to sing all the appropriate stanzas confidently, with heads up—not buried in the hymnal. It means a thoughtful consideration of the text; then a self-conscious singing of ideas rather than two- or four-measure musical phrases. Sometimes this calls for a quick breath where an idea ends in the middle of a musical phrase; sometimes it means binding two musical phrases together without a breath because the continuation of the ideas and words makes this appropriate ("Blest be the tie that binds Our hearts in Christian love"). It means rehearsal until the hymn can be sung with vitality and purposefulness. These are all skills that require serious preparation, but they are all within the power of any choir. When this is done, nothing needs to be said to the congregation by way of explanation or exhortation. The singing simply rises a level or two in the "hierarchy of values."

It is not at all necessary that the choir sing an anthem every week. It *is* necessary for the growth and health of the choir that its members feel a sense of achievement and purposefulness. For the struggling choir, unable to learn a new piece of music once a week, a self-consciousness about this important ministry to and through the congregation's singing can contribute to the necessary feeling that something important is being accomplished.

PROCESS OR PRODUCT?

A kind of conflict of values or priorities is intrinsic to the volunteer church choir situation. The reason for the choir's existence as commonly understood is to create a *product*—music—which will be used to enhance the worship experience. Very good—until one attempts to evaluate this task in the light of Scriptural teaching. The Bible does not directly address itself to matters of music or art or aesthetics. Furthermore, the New Testament offers no explicit directives as to the specific appropriate content of Christian worship.

Viewed, however, from another perspective, from the nature of the *process* that goes on as the choir works at its task, there is a great deal of Scriptural teaching that is relevant. Intrinsic to this process are matters of relationship—that which is going on between persons—and matters of attitude. There is no specific information in the Bible that will clearly support an opinion that a particular piece of music is good or bad, Christian or unchristian, more or less desirable as a part of worship. There is, however, a great deal of teaching that suggests that certain *attitudes* (for example, pride, sloth, anger) and certain aspects of interpersonal relationships (for example, love, indifference, hostility) are identifiably more or less Christian. It must be remembered that the church is not a building, an organization, a liturgy, or a body of music. It is the People of God—those persons who are aware of the living presence of God in Jesus Christ and who are committed to finding and doing his will. Therefore, the primary task of ministry is to be concerned with what happens in the lives of persons. The creation of buildings, organizations, liturgies, pieces of music, or musical organizations may be of great importance. But they should never, themselves, transcend concern for persons as the highest ministry of the church. Measured in terms of Christian values, the process in which the choir is involved should be, appropriately, a matter of greater concern than the music itself.

This distinction is difficult to communicate without seeming to say that sincerity or some other similar attitude can take the place of musical discipline. Not at all! Rather, it suggests the context in which the disciplines of music will be encountered; it establishes the ultimate determinative priorities for the whole operation.

To illustrate, when the primary emphasis is on the creation of a *product* any of the following phenomena may be present:

1. Persons are valued primarily for their ability to create the product. Thus good singers are more valuable than average ones and are often allowed privileges (coming late, missing rehearsals, etc.). Poor singers can easily be discarded as being of little use.

2. Expressions of intolerance, impatience, frustration, and sarcasm on the part of the director may be

acceptable and excusable if they help in driving the choir to better musical performance.

3. Additional competent singers may be brought into any performance situation if they can improve the product at that moment. Their lack of previous relationship to the choir community is irrelevant.

4. The feelings of individual choir members are less important than the music that the director can draw out of them. If the performance is good, then it is unimportant that singers may feel inadequate, harried, perhaps unable to identify personally and deeply with the concepts about which they are singing.

5. The choir is evaluated solely by how it sounds rather than by what kind of experience it is providing for its members.

When the primary emphasis is on the *process* a different set of characteristics will be observed. They may include any of these:

1. Singers are valued as persons. This does not mean that the nonsinger will necessarily be kept as part of the choir. It does mean that earnest and perhaps lengthy efforts will be made to help such persons become productive members of the group if they so desire. The ultimate musical objectives will be the same as in a product-oriented operation; the time taken and procedures involved in achieving these objectives may be different.

2. The director's attitudes will be constructive and affirming of persons. This will include honest facing of matters of musical competence and of commitment to the group. This assumes that a truly Christian relationship does not invite the concealing of problems but rather suggests that they be faced openly in honesty and love and mutual respect.

3. The music brought into Sunday's worship service will be the public sharing of that which is happening both musically and in areas of Christian growth within the choir. Therefore, if a choice must be made, the growth experience in rehearsal is of greater importance than the time of performance. This means that a singer who is absent on Sunday misses only a brief moment of ministry; one who is absent from rehearsal misses a variety of experiences which may have important long-range musical and personal consequences. In reality, this kind of climate within the choir tends to nurture a kind of faithful involvement where neither Sunday nor rehearsal is missed.

4. Because the performance is the sharing of what is happening within the group, it is inappropriate frequently and casually to bring in other singers to meet performance needs of the moment. Thus, each member of the group is important to it and also is responsible for what it does musically.

5. It will be recognized that the feelings of the individual singers about the music they sing will ultimately determine the value of that singing. Therefore, their response to the learning process will be a matter of serious concern. This may mean, for example, rehearsing an anthem for six or eight weeks instead of one or two so that the singers can feel comfortable with it and can make it their personal expression.

6. An important factor in the choice of music will be the consideration of how a particular anthem will contribute to the musical growth and the spiritual maturation of the choir members.

Giving priority to the process does not mean abandoning the desire for musical excellence. If the process is a good one, it will lead inevitably to the creation of good music. The achievement of this, in such a case, will not be at the expense of persons who are being exploited for what they can provide. Rather, it will come as the result of an emerging, disciplined, redemptive community that is living out and modeling the meaning of being "Christian."

WAR DEPARTMENT OR CENTER OF UNITY?

There is a paradoxical aspect to the role a choir may have within a church. On the one hand, in many churches the choir is the visible center of strength and unity. It will include the most active, faithful, concerned members of the congregation. During times of stress or change, for example, in an interim between pastors, its influence will be remarkably stabilizing and energizing. On the other hand is the situation in which the choir is known as the "war department" or the "battleground of the church." Within it is found a self-serving climate characterized by jealousy, peevishness, bickering, and loveless criticism. These attitudes may be visible in all relationships—those of persons within the group, of the choir toward the rest of the church, and, often, of the director toward the rest of the staff. What are the factors that encourage development in one or the other of these two directions?

A simplistic response would suggest that one group is more "spiritual" than the other. In a deep sense this is so. However, the "battleground" situation can exist even though outward attitudes and practices of piety are emphasized. Recruitment that focuses on participation as one's reasonable, expected response to God's great love; emphasis on Christian commitment as motivation for faithful and punctual involvement; the spending of much time in prayer by the group—these will not guarantee unity. Other dynamics are at work and need to be recognized.

When the director of the choir operates from different objectives than those of the pastor and/or the church, it is inevitable that dysfunctional tensions will develop. This seems obvious; it would be unreasonable for a church to enter into such a relationshp. However, there are subtle pressures that tend to obscure potential differences. When a church is in need of a choir director the most obvious criterion for selection is musical competence and experience. A second has to do with commitment to the whole Christian enterprise—to Christ. It is possible to observe competence and discuss commitment without ever identifying and exposing basic differences of understanding.

For example, a musician's professional training will inevitably tend to lead toward a product-centered objective. Anything that has to do with the use of music in worship or the relationship of the choir to other church activities will be viewed in the light of this primary objective. But there are limits to the time, energy, and money that is available, and competing claims upon them. In such a situation the attitude of both director and choir member toward persons or policies that interfere with the achieving of *their* objectives may easily become critical and intolerant. Furthermore, within the choir itself the giving of primary emphasis to the product encourages the development of undesirable attitudes. The contribution of some persons is obviously more useful than that of others in achieving this goal. Awareness of this leads to heightened or diminished assessments of personal worth, competition, jealousy, or envy.

Another area of potential difference between director and church or pastor may have to do with varying concepts of churchmanship or of worship. A church's need for a professionally competent musician or a director's desire for a position wherein he or she can use musicianship often overrides serious consideration of such differences. Thus the musician may be in a situation where he or she is asked to support kinds of music, or styles of worship, or theological understandings which are at best barely tolerated and, at worst, openly scorned. The enticement of the musical aspect of the situation may allow such a relationship to continue even though it is intrinsically dysfunctional. Likewise, a choir member may continue as part of the group because of musical interests through remaining disinterested or even hostile to the nonmusical aspects of the situation. In either of these eventualities, focus upon the purely musical or product element tends to heighten the problems. Conversely, attention to the relational or process element in the situation invites awareness, reflection, conversation, and positive change.

When a higher value is placed upon what a choir *is* than upon what it produces, it is possible that the choir may become a model of what "Christian community" truly means. Developing the skills of singing will then be accompanied by self-conscious efforts better to understand and live by the Christian faith. All of this will be in a context in which understanding and affirming one another is accepted as important. The problems that are inherent in such a task-oriented group do not disappear but, rather, will provide the occasion for working out ways in which commitment to the gospel can affect the situations found in everyday life. The learning of music is still the basic agenda of the rehearsal. However, this learning encompasses more than matters of pitch, choral tone, phonetics, and precision. It extends beyond these to the ideas that are being expressed through the music. Their meaning and content is discussed; the question of personal commitment to them is constantly a relevant one. All of this was suggested or implied in the discussion of the "process vs. product" concept of the choir. It is mentioned again here as we seek to examine the cause of a choir's becoming a center either of conflict or of Christian unity and maturity.

The dynamics that lead to unity or conflict operate with unique intensity because of the characteristic nature of the choir situation. Choir members are probably more continually and frequently engaged in their activity than members of any other group within the church. Normally they meet at least twice every week, for both rehearsal and ministry. The focus of all these meetings will be upon whatever objective they have determined for themselves. This intensive commitment to a task leads, predictably, to a heightened level of feelings about it. Thus there is a tendency that if the choir is divisive, it will be strongly so; if unified, the unity will be a powerful one.

The purpose in raising these issues is not to suggest an ideal model for a church choir. Rather, it is to suggest an agenda for conversation, discussion, or argument(?) between pastor and musician. It is not essential that these two share the same convictions about all these matters; it is of great importance that they identify the kinds and degree of differences that are present in their understandings and objectives. Each may have resources to bring to a relationship that can stimulate, inform, and perhaps alter the thinking of the other at some point. The tragedy is that in so many churches this effort to move toward mutual understanding and growth is never made. Such an effort will probably be costly in terms of *good!* time and energy and emotions—but that's what the ministry is all about.

Four

THE ORGAN

Church organs call to mind an incredible variety of instruments and instrumentalists. It is deceptive to use the same terms to describe them all, yet we do. At one extreme is the magnificent half-a-million-dollar instrument, located in an inspiring cathedral-like setting, played by an artist. At the other is the electronic spinet with its two half-keyboards and thirteen pedal notes with all of the sound coming from a small speaker by the organist's knee. The organist may be Aunt Suzy, whose dedication is remarkable. She may be a longtime pianist whose organ instruction is limited to the five free lessons that came with the instrument, and whose sense of rhythm is nonexistent. The immediate question is whether these two extremes have anything at all in common.

There are some things that are appropriate and possible for both cathedral and chapel. Others are characteristic of one but should not be attempted in the other. It is imperative for the pastor and the organist each to recognize both the potential and the limitations of their situation. They must come to terms, not with those conditions which they would like to have, but with those which actually exist.

THE ORGAN AND CONGREGATIONAL SINGING

For any organist of any level of competence, playing an instrument of whatever size, the primary task of ministry is to support the congregation as it sings. Achieving this goal begins with recognizing and accepting the absolute priority of congregational singing. As with the choir, this means commitment of a substantial amount of time and energy to the rehearsal of hymns. Aunt Suzy can make no greater contribution to the ministry of music in her church than that of leading a congregational hymn from the organ (or piano), introducing it with confidence, playing with authority, establishing and maintaining an appropriate tempo. However, this may be asking the impossible. It will certainly be so if she has only a few hours to prepare the hymns for Sunday, or if she fails to understand the importance of such preparation. For her to take this task seriously, she must see a high level of concern on the part of the pastor. There must be a visible awareness of her problems, coupled with planning and encouragement as they work together. The first step, obviously, is to choose the hymns several weeks ahead so they can be adequately rehearsed. In addition to practicing specific hymns as needed, the organist at any level of competence should be working continually to acquire and expand the various skills involved in supporting congregational singing.

For the advanced musician, the problem will not be the inability to play a hymn. More likely it will be a lack of interest which shows up in carelessness or simply in failure to use the full possible variety of professional skills in this activity. There may also be an attendant lack of identification with the singers, evidenced, for example, by setting an impossibly fast or slow tempo for purely musical reasons without regard to the fact that the worshipers simply cannot sing at that speed.

Once the organist can play the hymn as written with competence and confidence, another kind of support is possible. There are ways in which the singing of a hymn can be enhanced by judicious use of organ elaborations. One of these is the use of a "free accompaniment" on one or two stanzas which the congregation sings in unison. Another is the insertion of a modulation, perhaps with a brief interlude, before a final climactic stanza. Things of this nature must be done sensitively, skillfully, and occasionally. If done too infrequently, they will serve only to confuse the congregation and to give the impression that the organist likes to show off. Such ventures have within them a precarious element, but when well done can contribute a sense of gratification and excitement. In addition, they offer a partial antidote to the problem of thoughtless, superficial involvement on the part of the congregation which was identified in Chapter 2, "The Music of the Congregation."

If such experiences are new to the congregation, two things must happen in order for them to succeed. First, the worshipers must know what is expected of them. This may be done by identifying unison stanzas in the order of service, or by having an occasional brief congregational rehearsal, perhaps five minutes before the service begins. Congregations can and do become quite comfortable with such musical practices. Second, the members of the congregation need some understanding as to *why* such things are being done. Without this, many will perceive such an experience as simply the musician's attempt to be clever. Much resistance to innovation in worship is rooted in simple lack of understanding as to why such change might be worthwhile. Worshipers rightfully resist novelty that appears to be without purpose and seems to be included simply for the sake of newness. Conversely, they respond more positively to that which is perceived as reasonable and purposeful.

One further comment on the ministry of the organ in serving congregational singing concerns the frequent use of hymn materials for preludes, offertories, and postludes. For the organist of limited skill, it is more sensible to focus on hymn tunes as they appear in the hymnal, or on very simple arrangements of them, than to rely on simplistic nondescript pieces. Someone's "Meditation in B Flat" offers neither musical satisfaction nor associated meanings. For the accomplished musician the possibility is at hand to do as Bach did with his chorale preludes, that is, to take a familiar hymn tune and present it in a larger setting which can give new awareness, excitement, and meaning. This kind of music should be part of the repertoire of any organist capable of playing it.

"WORSHIP BEGINS WITH THE FIRST NOTE . . ."

Next Sunday morning most worship services will begin with a brief period of music played by the organist or the pianist. As with so many other aspects of church music, there may be a wide variety of objectives and expectations for this within a congregation. Many simply accept it without thought as being the way formal church worship always begins. For them it is a signal or a symbol;

its content or further purpose is not really important. It
announces the beginning of worship, and people hearing
the sound begin to congregate. It is at this point that the
conflict of expectations sets in.

Some individuals see this time as the occasion for ex-
changing greetings with friends. Occasionally the organ
music gets so loud as to make this difficult, and they wish
the organist could be more considerate and a bit less
demonstrative. After all, isn't the fellowship of the members of the body an important part of Christian worship?

Other worshipers find themselves disturbed, even a
bit annoyed, by these insensitive persons whose chatter
intrudes upon their attempts to be quiet and reflective
before the Lord. Their uneasiness may also be increased
occasionally by the loudness of the music or the nature
of some of it. After all, this is not the time for conversation or for music that is too highbrow, overpowering,
frivolous, or secular. It's the time to be quiet—to enter
into a more reverent frame of mind.

The organist is also offended by the amount of
thoughtless talking that goes on during the prelude. This
shows a lack of appreciation for the music which has
involved such diligent preparation. It certainly demonstrates a lack of reverence for the house and worship of
God. Any questioning of the repertoire used or the way
it is played is probably a reflection of unenlightened musical taste. After all, having spent many years in professional study, the organist knows that music has unique
power to communicate the greatness of God, if people
will only listen. Furthermore, the "better" the music is,
the more godliness it will instill.

The minister hopes that a reverent mood will have
been established by the time he or she enters the sanctu-

ary at the end of the prelude. After all, the minister feels that this is so important that he or she always begins the printed order of service with some reminder such as, "Our service begins with the first notes of the organ," or "The worship period begins when the prelude starts. After this, whisper only to God," or "Let the reverent tones of the organ prelude still our voices, that we may hear the voice of Him whom we have come to worship."

Again, the situations that I have just described are something of a caricature. Many ministers and organists have other expectations for worship itself and for the prelude that begins it. However, even in the best of situations there may be total lack of thought or a variety of thoughts concerning the prelude; these may exist to such a degree that its highest usefulness is hindered. As with other aspects of the ministry of music, the primary problem is not that several people have the wrong understanding. It is, rather, that several understandings exist and are in conflict with one another.

The following are four somewhat different ways of understanding and using the organ prelude. Each is appropriate in its own way:

1. *As Signal.* The prelude exists simply to announce that the worship service is about to begin. It is probably brief, and not affected adversely by conversation since it is primarily a signal rather than something to invite attentive listening and response. The repertoire involved may be anything within the competence of the organist that is not grossly or obviously inappropriate. For most members of the congregation this will not be a time of worship but truly a prelude to worship. In such a situation, a suggestion preceding the order of service asking for the

congregation's silent and attentive attitude would be unreal and inappropriate.

2. *As Mood Inducer.* The objective is to suggest through music certain patterns of thought and emotion that are considered to be appropriate for corporate worship. At its worst, this is an attempt to compel people to assume an attitude that is artificial and unreal. (See the discussion on "Music as Mood" in Chapter 5, "Music and Worship.") It doesn't matter whether the attitude called for is one of reverence and sobriety or one of celebration and artificial joy; the offense, if there is one, lies in assuming that there is something about worship "in spirit and truth" that involves the striking of attitudes. At its best, this may be a cultic act that appropriately invites reflection and heightened awareness of the presence and purpose of God. It requires that attention be given to the music, whether it exists for the purpose of manipulation or of suggestion. With such an objective, most congregations will need to be reminded of the purpose of the prelude. This may be done through the bulletin, from the pulpit, or in any other way possible.

3. *As Worship Through Music.* This can best be illustrated by the cathedral setting where magnificence of architecture and glass, great organ resources, and a high level of musical skill combine to make possible an experience that is aesthetically and religiously moving. The prelude can be truly an encounter with God through the nonpropositional medium of music. Such an experience is not limited to a cathedral setting, but it does require an adequate organ, a competent organist, and good music. If the organ is a modest electronic one or the organist is a musician of limited capabilities, then it is

realistic not to expect too much. Worship will not occur simply because we desire it or say that we are having it. Attentiveness to the music on the part of the worshiper is essential to achieve this objective. However, in this situation it is likely that such inspiring music will, itself, invite the appropriate response. Only an occasional hint or reminder might be necessary. A sentence such as those above would certainly not be inappropriate though perhaps not necessary.

4. *As Worship Through Ideas.* The operative element here is neither the mood of the music nor its great beauty, but rather in related ideas—those of texts that are associated with particular recognizable music. These will most often be the texts of hymns, but may also be those of familiar pop or secular music. Some churches make use of the latter by supplementing or even replacing the organ prelude with recordings or tapes. In any case, the objective is to suggest to the congregation some ideas that will relate in some fashion to the total worship experience of the morning. Such music may provide the opportunity for encounter with God, with self, or with the world and as such may truly be the occasion of worship. The response will not be to the sheer beauty of music. Rather, it will require giving thought and attention on the part of the worshipers to ideas and related associations.

A few comments about these different understandings may be in order.

a. Although these four views are not discrete and isolated from each other, several (1 vs. 2 or 3) are mutually exclusive.

b. The church of limited resources has no reasonable

possibility of operating at level 3, "As Worship Through Music."

c. When the prelude is functioning at level 3 or 4, a question arises. If this is part of the actual experience of worship rather than simply the prelude to it, why should the choir and ministers not participate in it? If the worship truly begins "with the first note of the organ," then should it not be the worship of all? To have these persons enter at a later time is a bit like having a song service "before we begin the meeting."

Some churches have found it possible to combine several of these functions advantageously. There might be a brief prelude serving as "signal," after which choir and worship leaders would enter. This would be followed by the giving of announcements and a call to worship by pastor or choir. Then, with all participants present and attentive, some organ or other instrumental music, carefully chosen and functioning at level 3 or 4, could be shared by all as truly the beginning of worship. This music will be particularly effective for the largest number of worshipers if it can be related to something ideological, perhaps a passage of Scripture or a hymn text.

d. If the organist perceives the prelude as functioning at level 3, while the pastor's expectation is directed at 2 and the congregation's at 1, then a situation of inherent confusion exists. It is better to attempt to bring these expectations together at a realistic point of common focus.

Finding such common ground begins with conversation about the matter between the staff members who are involved. These participants may have emotional commitment to one of these positions without ever having thought through its implications. Even if they have done so, their convictions need to be compared with those differing ones held by co-workers. It isn't imperative that a unanimously accepted view be achieved. It is important that each person sharing in this particular ministry begins to understand what is valued by the others. It is important that discussion take place as to how to respond to the concerns of each. At some point the congregation needs to be brought into this consideration, perhaps through discussion of expectations in small groups (for example, the worship committee). It should eventually lead to explanation and reminder as needed for the worshiping congregation.

In I Cor., ch. 14, Paul underscores the fact that as members of Christ's body, we will have differences. The other emphasis of the passage is equally important—that we must recognize and affirm these differences and find out how to bring them together under the headship of Christ.

MUSICAL WALLPAPER

There is a familiar story, perhaps apocryphal, about a noted American organist who was asked by the pastor to "just play something" to cover a moment of delay in the course of a worship service. He is reported to have whispered back, "Why don't you just mumble something?" The obvious point has to do with the thoughtless mechanistic use of music. We tend to do this as easily with organ music as with congregational singing. There is another matter involved, however, which is the issue under consideration here. It has to do with the worshiping church's fear of silence.

In the environment of our daily life we recognize the

dysfunctional element of noise pollution. We occasionally complain about the ubiquitous "musical wallpaper" —that constant background sound which is characteristic of our society—yet we attempt to plaster over every crack of silence that threatens the continuity of our worship. Our apprehension is as if we were in some way like an invisible radio station that needs constantly to reassure its listeners that it is still on the air. We seem to need to maintain an aural continuity lest the casual listener be diverted to something else.

This practice fails to recognize that silence, though a rare event in the context of today's society, can be desirable. It overlooks the possibility that silence may be a dynamic rather than a passive condition—one in which the interrelationship of persons within a community may be powerfully sensed. The Quakers have known this for many centuries. The suggestion has been made that in silence the majesty of God may be uniquely apprehended.[17] Yet ignoring this, we expect worship to be a reflection of the activism and continual external stimulation of twentieth-century life. We react to silence as if it were a signal that something has gone wrong; thus we miss experiencing its creative possibilities.

If, for example, a time for personal silent prayer is felt to be desirable in worship, then pastor and organist can best minister by allowing a period of unbroken silence. If the organist intrudes into this silence by playing some neutral music without recognizable related text, then this "Christian Muzak" destroys the value and power of absolute silence. If a familiar hymn is played, then the associational factors discussed above will tend to operate. While the pastor has suggested that the prayer be personal and individual, the organist insists on calling to mind a particular hymn text which suggests or becomes the content of prayer. Both individualized prayer and corporate prayer, guided and focused by a hymn text, can be appropriate and worthwhile in worship. The point is simply that they are different experiences, separate from and incompatible with each other. In this, as with other issues we have considered, it is important that both minister and musician share the same objectives.

If a congregation is not accustomed to times of silence, then its members may need help in knowing just what to do with it. In such a situation, after perhaps fifteen seconds of silent prayer, worshipers begin to shift from the experience of prayer to that of anxiety. Heads lift covertly and eyes open to see whether the pastor has had a heart attack or has vanished from the sanctuary. If silence is to be used in any new way, the congregation needs a word of guidance and reassurance. It needs to know what to expect as to duration and it needs suggestions as to how to use that silence.[18]

There is a place both for silence and for judicious competent offering of musical suggestions and connectives by the organist. If technical competence is limited, then less use of background or interludes is indicated. If professional skill is ample, then the opportunity is at hand to choose to make both sound and silence meaningful.

The three issues that have been dealt with in this chapter are relevant for the organist and the pastor of any size church, large or small. The primacy of congregational singing implies two things. First, it identifies a priority of objective and evaluation. Second, it identifies a task whose successful accomplishing is within the realistic possibility of the relatively unsophisticated organist. The matters discussed concerning the role of the organ prelude can be extended to suggest ways of viewing the offertory and postlude. The question of Why? is equally appropriate concerning each of these functions. The answer to this question is all too frequently assumed by both organist and pastor, unfortunately with several conflicting assumptions present in a given situation.

Commonly the issue of the relative functions of music and silence may be resolved unilaterally, by directives from the pastor or by the continuing of customary practices by the organist. Whatever the source of the decision, if it is made without awareness of the issues involved and discussion of them, its consequences may be at best thoughtless persistence and at worst the source of frustration and tension.

As in the other areas of the ministry of music that we have considered, it is from the point where organist, music director, and pastor meet to consider purposes and differences that healthy and creative ministry can emerge. Each one needs to reach out to the others with the invitation, "Let's discuss it."

Five

MUSIC
AND WORSHIP

Why use music in worship? We have considered the music of the congregation, the choir, and the organ without raising the basic question, Why use music at all? This also must be answered if we are properly to identify objectives and expectations.

It is difficult to find simple, direct Scriptural answers to this question. The Old Testament offers the example of a Levitical musical system as part of temple worship, and includes a few specific exhortations, such as Psalm 150. Mention of music in the New Testament is limited to a few comments about congregational singing or examples of it. Nowhere does one find explicit teaching as to why we should have music, what that music should be, or how it should be used.

The history of the church shows no consensus concerning the role of music. Prior to the Renaissance, the church was the center of musical development. It was in the monasteries that formal musical styles developed and musical notation was invented. In the Middle Ages our question might have been answered by saying, "It is in the church that music is nurtured as an enriching part of human experience." But by the time of the Reformation, music was finding a life of its own outside of ecclesiastical circles. Within the new Protestant churches an incredible variety of usages were emerging. Calvin's response to the minimal Scriptural teaching was to say, "Don't use it (music in any form) unless it is specifically enjoined." Luther's response was exactly the opposite: "It is in the realm of 'adiaphora' (i.e., that area left to conscience because of the absence of specific Biblical teaching). Use what you will that seems appropriate." In early post-Reformation times, the spectrum of belief and practice within Protestantism extended from the rejection of all music in worship (early Quakers) through the very limited congregational singing of psalms without instruments (strict Calvinism) to the acceptance of organ and choirs (Lutheran and Anglican).

There has been no commonly accepted expectation of musical excellence and sophistication. The village choir (mentioned in Chapter 3, "The Choir") usually offered music of a modest level of competence. In contrast to this, the eighteenth-century church music of Bach, involving congregation, choir, soloists, organ, and instruments, showed a high degree of musical creativity and competence. However, by the nineteenth century the center of this creativity had moved from the church to the concert hall and music conservatory, although in certain churches of a variety of denominations excellent vocal and instrumental performance could still be found. The pipe organ still retains its distinctive identification with the church (in spite of a generation in which it provided entertainment in the movie houses). Nineteenth-century mass evangelism added a new element. It was accompanied by a concept of church music that included large choirs (several thousand singers) and congregational music that was essentially popular and colloquial in style. To this expression (the gospel song) which still persists today has been added the ventures of pop-related music which significantly emerged in the church in the late 1960's. These experiments were not limited to any denomination or style of churchmanship, but rather they involved a major part of the Christian community and a wide variety of idioms.

Listing this variety of musical use is not for the purpose of providing a thumbnail sketch of the history of church music. It is to indicate that it is impossible to identify, within the church's history, a common philosophy and practice of music.

Neither Scripture nor history offers a simple or direct answer to our question Why? Let us, then, attempt to get at the issue quite differently. We will approach the matter pragmatically, identifying and examining five differing (and sometimes contradictory) ways in which music can function.

Music as Participation

One of the most basic functions of church music is to involve persons in the making of it. This view is primarily concerned with the experience of the whole congregation as participants, secondarily with the choir, and minimally with individual soloists or performers.

The value central to this concept is active involvement in a situation rather than passive observation of it—to be engaged as a participant rather than somewhat removed from the action as a spectator. Participation in congregational music can encourage the worshiper to be truly

what that term implies—one who worships. At least such
involvement makes it more difficult to sleep through the
service.

A second aspect of participation in making music can
be identified by the word "reinforcement." This deals
with the difference between thinking "I love you" and
saying "I love you." Never mind, here, that saying this
still falls short of engaging in appropriate behavior. That
is another issue. Whenever "Our God, Our Help in Ages
Past" is thoughtfully sung, the weight and meaning of its
message is worked more deeply into the worshiper's
sense of identity and purpose.

Closely related to this process of reinforcement is that
of learning and remembering. In Deut., ch. 31, the Scriptures record a conversation between God and Moses in
which God says to Moses, "Now therefore write this
song, and teach it to the people of Israel." As they become possessed by self-interest and turn to other gods,
"this song shall confront them as a witness." This is the
process that operates as the insidious devices of rhyme
and meter and melody and repetition serve to lodge
Christian truth deeply within a person's life. It is because
of the potential importance of this process that serious
attention should be given to the functional and theological content of the songs that become part of the furniture
of one's mind through participation in church music.

Still another related element is that of being involved
in an activity that is both common to the group and
distinctive of it. The singing of "Blest Be the Tie That
Binds" at the Lord's Supper, or of "We Shall Overcome"
in a civil rights march of the 1960's, both serve in similar
fashion to identify and strengthen the commitment of
each person to the common purpose of the group. Doing

this draws attention to the common bond that holds the group together. This common bond is further strengthened if it finds expression through characteristic and uniquely distinctive actions even though these serve to irritate persons outside the fellowship. For centuries, the term "psalm-singing Christians" has been used as an epithet by those outside the group to describe those within it. It is irrelevant here that such a stigma may be grounded in matters of hypocritical living or of a lifestyle that substitutes speech (singing) for action. Beyond these negative aspects lies a deeper dynamic whereby hymn singing gives identity to one group, the church, at the same time that it communicates a sense of otherness to persons outside that group. This is consistent with the gospel. There *is* a difference between those who are of the church and those who are not. Our openness to those outside the fellowship should not obscure this difference.

Finally, there is the concept of "process vs. product," which was identified and discussed in Chapter 3, "The Choir." Reiteration of this concept is appropriate as we consider the participatory aspect of church music. The experience of sharing in the interaction of a group (a choir) that truly exists as a redemptive ministering fellowship might provide adequate reason for the valuing of this participatory aspect.

Music as Commentary

Frequently, church music exists in relationship to a text. Such is the case with a hymn, an anthem, a solo. This relationship may be simply functional. In some instances —for example, the use of a nondistinctive psalm tune— the music serves primarily as a vehicle for the text. It exists essentially in order that a group (congregation or choir) might simultaneously sing that text. This functions as a pleasant variation of reading the text aloud together. The tune is without distinctive characteristics and serves equally well for a variety of texts. In this situation the role of the music is mainly utilitarian. It is completely at the service of the text.

At the opposite extreme is that practice found among many of the Baroque composers and their nineteenth-century imitators in which the primary objective was the expression of musical phrases and patterns. Within the worst of such music, text may be nonsensically repetitive. It may become meaningless, with each syllable serving simply as a means by which to project the musical line or structure. Somewhere between these two extremes is the majority of vocal music in which text and music exist side by side with the hopeful expectation that in some manner the music will give a distinctive meaning or coloration to the text; that it will, in other words, offer a commentary on it.

When choir or soloist is involved, the proper functioning of this process may be lost when either too little or too much attention is given to communicating the text intelligibly. When too little, obviously the ideological focus of the music's commentary is lost. In the other direction, it is possible (though uncommon) to be so preoccupied with the text that damage results to the sound and flow of the music. If the text is all that matters, it would be far better simply to have someone step to the pulpit and read the words. It is the fusion of the two which is the objective—the words to express ideas or content and the music to provide commentary, to suggest implications and additional levels of meaning.

When both composer and interpreter operate with a high level of skill and inspiration, this exposition of the text by the music can be remarkably effective. The theologian Oscar Cullmann has said concerning this process:

> Johann Sebastian Bach has made it possible for us to hear the musical interpretation of the words of this ancient creed · [the *Credo* of the B Minor Mass] which faithfully reproduces the New Testament faith in Christ's resurrection and our own. . . . And Handel in the last part of "The Messiah" gives us some inkling of what St. Paul understood by the sleep of those who rest in Christ. . . . Whether we share this hope or not, let us at least admit that in this case the artists have proved the best expositors of the Bible.[19]

If this is true, we must take seriously the possibility that a better understanding of a text may come when it is encountered in an appropriate musical setting. At this point, it is conceivable that the musician may share with the preacher the ministry of helping the Word to become clear and alive.[20]

In congregational music, the operation of this process can be seen, for example, in the difference given to the hymn text "Jesus, Lover of My Soul" when it is sung to the tune "Martyn" as contrasted to "Aberystwyth." Or consider "For All the Saints Who from Their Labors Rest," as sung to "Sarum" or to "Sine Nomine." In both cases the first tune is gentle, passive, comfortable, while the second is powerful, driving, dynamic. The difference in the character of the tunes suggests a similar different meaning for the text itself as one or the other is used to express it.

For the organist or instrumentalist this aspect of music is severely limited. It can occasionally take place when the music played is a development of a familiar hymn tune which, in turn, suggests a specific text. "Amazing Grace" as sung in America would exemplify this, or "A Mighty Fortress Is Our God."

In the category previously considered, that of "Participation," the matter of musical skill was not of great importance; rather, it was involvement in the making of music that mattered. However, when the objective is the functioning of music to provide commentary, a reasonably high level of musical competence is imperative. This process simply does not work when the attention of the listener is diverted from the ideas expressed by the music to the problems of musical production.

MUSIC AS EXHORTATION

This function is virtually limited to certain kinds of vocal solos and choral anthems. While there are hymns whose texts are literally words of exhortation (for example, "Rise Up, O Men of God!" "Praise Ye the Lord, the Almighty, the King of Creation"), the dynamic actually functioning when they are sung is most likely that of participation. There is, however, a group of solos, quartets, and anthems whose objective is frankly exhortation. These have developed in the context of mass evangelism. They combine expressions of personal testimony with the invitation for the listener to enter into a similar experience with Christ. At this point the singer or choir is actually sharing in or doing the task of preacher or evangelist. In such a situation, the function of the music is to provide an appealing vehicle for the message. The matter of musical competence is relevant but not as determinative as in the previous category.

MUSIC AS MOOD

Our common experience with television and the cinema makes us familiar with the power that music has to touch the essence of the moment on the screen. When it works, it comments on the action and emotions behind that action as words or pictures seldom can. When used with sensitivity, it can communicate with great richness the variety of human emotions, suggesting rage, tenderness, despair, or fear with equal power. This is what has been implied above in viewing music in its function as commentary. However, we probably have also experienced the degeneration of this process through heavy-handed excess wherein the creative use of music has been replaced by the utilization of a series of manipulative symbols. Soon, on the screen or on television, we learn that love is a violin, modern jazz means trouble in the streets, war is brass with cymbals, both worry and fear are cellos, and God is the Hollywood Bowl Symphony Orchestra.[21]

These same processes are at work as we use music in worship. When the desired function of the music is to create a *feeling* of reverence or celebration; when the minister says, "I like good music because it gets people ready for my sermon"; when the organ plays quietly beneath the devotional parts of the service such as prayer or Communion; when the choir hums sweetly and softly during a time of invitation; then we are in this dangerous and elusive but important territory where music is being used to create mood.

There is a potential problem here and it is one of great subtlety. It emerges by shifting the focus of attention

from matters of faith to the feelings that might appropriately result from such faith. This questionable striving to
induce a particular feeling as a desirable end in itself may
be done openly or covertly.

The overt approach can be expressed by the phrase
"the danger of striking attitudes in worship."[22] Traditionally we have assumed that certain attitudes should
characterize Christian worship. The commonest of these
has been reverence. Children were taught to approach
the house of God with proper reverence; we were encouraged to come to worship with appropriate quiet and
sobriety. Leaders of the service were expected to function with dignity. Of course the music should emphasize
these attitudes and should avoid any hint of lightness or
frivolity that might be incompatible with such a mood.
This attitude of reverence, it was felt, could best be nurtured by a distinctive kind of music—one completely
without secular associations. Thus Archibald Davison
has written:

> The finest church music suggests the church and nothing
> outside of it, for that music is not sensuous or emotional as
> is the music of our secular world. . . . One need but ask
> himself, "Is this the music of my everyday world? Is its
> language familiar to me in many forms? [That's bad.] Or is
> it a speech apart; remote, archaic perhaps, sacerdotal,
> strange; a language to which the church alone would be
> hospitable?" [That's good.][23]

The strangeness of such music and its association with
the experience of worship and with nothing else was
desirable in that these characteristics contributed to this
feeling of mystery and reverence.

Today the mood has changed—literally. As a reaction

to dreary seeking after reverence and solemnity, and in response to intrinsic characteristics of the gospel, the church has seized on the mood of celebration as that which is appropriate for today. This concept, while having an authentic element, leads easily to the same perversion as did the striving for reverence. Celebration is sought as a feeling that should be induced rather than accepted as a consequence of true worship.

We would do well to be guided here by the dictionary definitions of "celebration" which place the emphasis upon *remembering* rather than upon feelings. Scripture is full of this kind of celebration—for example, Ex., ch. 15; Deut., ch. 32; Ps. 113 to 118. To celebrate in these terms is not to hang a banner, strum a guitar, or blow up some balloons and give three cheers for Jesus. It is, rather, to remember who God is and what he has done. It is the remembrance of his mighty acts and the fresh awareness of their meaning for today that, if given opportunity, leads to confidence and hope, courage and anticipation, excitement and joy, and true peace.

In congregational music we often encounter this attempt to seek a particular emotion or feeling. Many of our hymnals include a word of instruction above each hymn suggesting how it is to be sung. The congregation is invited to sing "devotionally" or "reverently" or "with dignity" or "joyfully." These are all moods or feelings that might appropriately accompany worship "in spirit and truth." The subtle problem here is important though difficult to get hold of. It lies in the attempt to seek the feeling first as something valuable in itself. In the words of Dr. Routley, these directions for hymn singing could really be considered as "directions for what expression of face to wear while singing." That's not the same as being aware of what might happen when truth is grasped and expressed in fresh and new ways.

To approach worship this way is to confuse cause and effect. To place the emphasis on creating a particular feeling or mood diverts it from its proper focus which is God and his revelation in Jesus Christ. Note in the New Testament the remarkable absence of concern about subjective feelings. Note that the evangelical sermons recorded there rarely emphasize personal feeling or personal testimony. Rather, they invite attention to God's work throughout history, to the events of the incarnation and the meaning of those events, and to an invitation to belief and faith and commitment. No concern there about feelings but rather preoccupation with the Object of feelings and with action that might result in feelings.

In his book *Church Music and Theology*, Erik Routley discusses that characteristic of Romanticism which he calls "the sin of loving the longing more than the thing."[24] It is not uncommon, particularly in church music, to encounter expressions that suggest that the condition of loving is more to be desired than Jesus himself; that peace and joy are the objects of our search rather than the living God. Once we yield to this way of perceiving, music offers us unlimited eloquence. Better than words or actions, music can suggest the *feelings* of love, or peace, or joy, or reverence. And, all too frequently, it suggestively entices us into thinking of these as the subject of ministry rather than the resultant of it.

The church musician or the pastor is in dangerous territory when he or she substitutes for the proclaiming of the gospel the striving for feelings which may be perfectly appropriate if they come as part of one's response to the gospel. When done openly in the "striking of attitudes" this may be rather harmless—perhaps a bit humorous. When done covertly as an attempt to manipulate a congregation into certain feelings, this practice deserves rebuke. Intrinsic to the method of Christ's ministry and the nature of the gospel itself is the fact that God invites persons to respond knowingly and freely to himself. It is incompatible with the gospel to attempt to bring about or contrive actions on the part of persons who think that such contrived responses are really expressions of their free relationship with him. In essence, such use of music can become the attempt to seize power over another and to compel a certain response. Dietrich Bonhoeffer, in addressing himself to this issue, called such a process "human absorption":

> It appears in all the forms of conversion wherever the superior power of one person is consciously or unconsciously misused to influence profoundly and draw into his spell another individual or a whole community. Here one soul operates directly upon another soul. The weak have been overcome by the strong, the resistance of the weak has broken down under the influence of another person. He had been overpowered, but not won over by the thing itself.[25]

The difficulty in even attempting to discuss this process lies in the impossibility of clearly defining it. Perhaps persuasion (an appropriate objective) slips over into manipulation (an inappropriate one) at the point where the motivating pressure is concealed. In any case, the point is not to suggest that the rational proclamation of truth should be divorced from feeling or emotion, but rather that the feeling or emotion should not be sought *instead* of rational encounter with God's truth. The church musician will find it pointless and impossible precisely to identify and categorize every use of music in terms of this issue. He or she *can* recognize in himself or herself, when it arises, the questionable tendency to choose and use and interpret music primarily for the effect it will have on the listener's response rather than for its excellence as a musical statement. At such a point he or she should take care.

MUSIC AS REVELATION

And then that man [the preacher] will have the congregation sing ancient songs full of weighty and weird memories, strange ghostly witnesses of the sufferings, struggles, and triumphs of the long departed Fathers, all leading to the edge of an immeasurable event, all, whether the minister and people understand what they are singing or not, full of reminiscences of God, always of God. "God is present!" God *is* present, the whole situation witnesses, cries, simply shouts of it, even when in minister or people there arises questioning, wretchedness, or despair.[26]

Beyond the kind of revelation that music can provide in its role as commentary is potentially another deep level of communication—one that may offer understanding and give meaning to faith that transcends theological formulations. As Barth has said above, this may be found in the hymnbook when it is understood as the timeless testimony of the saints, the church, the continuing body of Christ.

And we never sing to Him alone. There are always the saints who have gone before, the saints who sing by our sides, and the saints who will sing over our graves. They are always one, always in unison, always saying and singing that nothing can ever empty the world of the communion of saints.[27]

This weighty witness transcends the theological statements of any particular hymn. It is an affirmation and validation of God's continuing purposeful work with his people.

Barth, again, illuminates another aspect of church music—its ability to express the inexpressible. He says concerning the articulation of the incredible truth of the incarnation—the identifying of God with humanity:

> Words are hostile to it [the genuine miracle of Christmas], detrimental, always powerless to justify it. The man who undertakes to celebrate in *words* his own "elevated humanity" becomes all too easily confusing and incredible to himself. "All patterns are too stiff for me and all speech too tedious and cold." How fortunate that when we are disturbed and oppressed by the problem of words we can flee to the realm of music, to Christian music and to a musical Christianity! Exactly because of its lack of concepts, music is the true and legitimate bearer of the message of Christmas.[28]

This assumes the possibility that all understanding need not come solely through the medium of the spoken or printed word—in fact, cannot come that way. It suggests that our knowledge of God cannot be limited and bounded by what we *say* about him. Through the arts, especially through music, the transcendent, the ineffable, the incomprehensible may be encountered as God's Spirit brings revelation to our human spirit.

A word of caution, however. Beauty, goodness, and truth are values commonly recognized by humanity. Truly, they proceed from God, but they do not inevitably lead back to him. In a discussion of this issue, Jaroslav Pelikan has suggested: "In values, man has confronted an ultimate, perhaps even an absolute. Absolute Truth, the Highest Good, Ultimate Beauty are phrases which indicate that in the area of value there is something transcending—or at least something many have thought of as transcending—the relativities of ordinary existence." However, he continues, "value is not God and cannot be a fit object of worship." These values are not ends to be sought by the church but rather are means toward a greater End. "The very things which the natural mind makes the objects of its idolatrous worship become, for the mind of faith, instruments in the service of God."[29] The creating or the hearing of great music may be a "peak experience" (using the psychological terms of Abraham Maslow).[30] One may have this kind of experience without recognizing the living God as revealed by Jesus Christ through the mediation of the Holy Spirit.

There is always the possibility that God may break through to us, revealing himself through the ineffable. Remember the description of the dedication of Solomon's Temple as recorded in II Chron. 5:13f.: "When the song was raised, with trumpets and cymbals and other musical instruments, . . . the house of the LORD was filled with a cloud, so that the priests could not stand to minister because of the cloud; for the glory of the LORD filled the house of God."

In one sense, to try to identify and discuss discretely these different facets of church music is unrealistic. In reality, one dynamic may merge into another, several may be operating simultaneously, or no one may be obviously determinative. At this point we may well say, "So what?" How, then, does this catalog of categories affect function?

If objectives (possibilities) are identified, then, (1) differing objectives of pastor and musician can be reconciled or at least discussed; (2) evaluation can take place as to whether, in fact, objectives are being achieved; and (3) at least, better understanding of what is going on can lead to more intelligent action. Occasionally the appropriate question arising from this is whether certain assumed objectives could possibly be achieved in a specific situation; perhaps expectations should change. For example:

—The organist may be seeking something transcendent through the use of "good" music which, because of his or her limitations or those of the organ, cannot possibly be achieved. The transcendent potential of Bach's music can never be realized by playing a simplified transcription on an electronic spinet organ with two half-keyboards and thirteen pedal notes; neither is it a reality simply because the name "Bach" is printed in the order of service.

—The choir director may be seeking musical commentary on a particularly meaningful text which in fact, as usually sung, is unintelligible. Recognition of this intrinsic problem might lead to (a) printing the text in the order of worship, (b) serious, extensive work with the choir on phonating consonants until the text is really intelligible, (c) recognition and acceptance of the fact that a particular anthem may be so constructed that its text can never be intelligibly sung, therefore (d) discarding it, or accepting it as something whose primary value is in its being internalized by each choir member as part of the "process" aspect.

It is possible that in many situations none of the leaders have truly identified just what they are seeking. Such identification can be the beginning of a far more constructive approach to ministry.

A Postscript on Accepting Reality

Cathedral or chapel—which is the better style of worship? This question demands to be answered by another question. Better for what? The issue here is that of facing the reality that a chapel is *not* a cathedral. Neither is it 10 percent of a cathedral even though that figure might represent the relationship between the two as far as size of building and congregation is concerned. It is tempting for the pastor and the musician in the small church to take the cathedral as a model, either consciously or unconsciously. This might involve such expectations as assuming the presence of a choir, extensive use of the organ including repertoire by the "great" composers, inevitable programming of special music in worship by soloists and choir, attempts to nurture an awareness of God's transcendence, mystery, and awesomeness such as is fostered by soaring glass and stone, vast space, and majestic organ. These are not realistic expectations.

The uniqueness of the chapel lies in its offering the experience of worship in an intimate familylike environment. Formal liturgical and ceremonial elements are less important; these have their greatest value in expediting the experience of a large crowd. Worship can be highly personalized when it takes place in a small community where each worshiper is known to the other.

It is important to realize that chapel and cathedral potentially offer the worshiping Christian two quite different experiences. Wisdom lies in recognizing the validity and the limitations of each and in choosing to use the style appropriate to the situation in which one ministers.

Six

PLANNING
FOR WORSHIP

In many churches, planning for worship is a simple operation. The pastor, the choir director, and the organist simply take last week's bulletin, scratch out the hymns, anthems, and organ music identified there, insert the titles for the present week, and pass them on to the church secretary, who then prepares the next Sunday's order of worship. The pastor or the musician may keep a log of hymns divided into such categories as "opening hymns," "closing hymns," "prayer hymns." There the date of singing a particular hymn is recorded to prevent excessive use or omission of a particularly old and familiar friend. In similar fashion, the organist and the choir director work their way through the repertoire which they possess with the occasional addition of something new. On special festival days (Thanksgiving, Christmas, Easter) a particular focus or common emphasis will probably be visible.

In such a situation it may be that all the elements of the worship service are organized under a fixed series of headings (for example, Contemplation, Adoration, Supplication, Inspiration, Dedication) which would seem to indicate a thoughtful, meaningful progression. Unfortunately however, in practice the content of hymn, anthem, or responsive reading often fails to be related to the heading under which it is placed. Members of the congregation don't notice such inconsistency because they have become accustomed to it and the headings no longer have meaning. In such a manner, free-church worship may become more inflexible than that of liturgical denominations without gaining the advantages of logical progression and appropriateness that a carefully prepared liturgy can offer.

A more thoughtful consideration of how one might go about planning for worship begins with the attempt to answer one basic question: What do we expect to happen in worship?

WHAT HAPPENS IN WORSHIP?

One way of responding to this question is to seek to define the term "worship." Definitions exist in endless variety: "the act of paying divine honors; reverence, honor, respect to God"; "God's revelation to man and man's response to God"; "the habitual, purposeful, corporate referring of life to God"; "the corporate response of the congregation to the revelation of God in Jesus Christ"; "an encounter with God, self, and the world"; "the ascribing of 'worthship' to God." Any such definition may help to stimulate thought, but it is inadequate to communicate either the richness of the term or the variety of different ways in which we use it.

A different kind of response seeks to identify the dynamics of worship as we experience it in the form of a weekly cultic activity of the community which is the church. What is the rationale for including each item that is part of the worship service? What is the relationship of each to the others? It is possible to identify at least four different patterns or styles of worship, each of which reflects a particular understanding of these relationships.

1. *Variety*

□ – □ – □ – □ – □ – □ – □

In the above diagram of the variety pattern of worship, each square represents an item in the series of specific elements that make up the worship experience.

Each item stands alone. A flippant description of such a construct might be to call it a Christian variety show. Music, prayers, Scripture, preaching, announcements, all are programmed so as to provide a varied experience. Thus the service alternates between music and speech, standing and sitting, listening and responding. The pastor serves as master of ceremonies. The star attraction is the preacher delivering the sermon, and all else seeks to get the audience ready for that. In England this kind of service is sometimes identified by the delightful label "hymn sandwich." Its primary characteristic is that there is no visible rational basis for organization other than the principle of variety and the fact that everything is somehow related to God.

The weakness of such an approach is that it resists any attempt on the part of the worshipers to become thoughtfully involved. There is no apparent reason why one hymn rather than another follows the responsive reading; no logical relationship between a soprano solo and the prayer that precedes or follows it. There is no invitation or enticement to become actively and creatively involved with the progression of ideas—there is no progression of ideas. Since there is no way to anticipate what will come next and no point in thinking about it, the worshipers tend to respond by taking on a passive attitude upon entering church. For them, the best way to handle this situation is just to sit until told what to do next.

An attendant problem is that those who worship in such a situation may become highly resistant to change in any part of the service. The one secure and rational aspect of this service is its sheer predictability. The anthem *always* precedes the sermon; the Doxology *always* follows the offering; the responsive reading *always* comes after the first hymn and before the prayer. To alter this sequence is to weaken the worshipers' one secure link with it. No matter that there may be a good reason for such alteration. This congregation is not sensitive to reason in worship. Its members have been conditioned to do without it.

The redemption of such a situation is that God's Holy Spirit works anyhow, as and when he chooses. To fail to recognize this is to fail to understand the basic nature of Christian worship—worship is not simply human activity but, rather, an encounter with the living God. Recognition of this might provide a good rationale for the avoidance of any liturgy at all. Nevertheless, it is not an adequate reason for a thoughtless or careless approach to the planning of worship.

2. *Thematic*

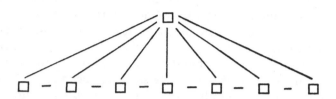

This model is similar to the first, with one addition. All the various activities of worship have a common focus; they deal with the same idea; they are painted with the same color. Every such service has its theme. An effort is made to express this theme in hymns, anthems, readings, prayers, and sermon. This is an attempt by the free church to do every Sunday what takes place in most churches on Christmas and Easter.

The advantage over the previous model is obvious. A rational element has been added. Should the worshipers desire to find some kind of purpose and coherence, it is now possible to organize and think about what is being experienced. Also, well-constructed services of this kind are good to have in order to be able to share them with other ministers who are able to appreciate fully the time and thought that went into their planning.

Unfortunately, this appreciation may come more easily from fellow pastors than from members of the congregation. Unless a great deal of effort is made to explicate the theme of the day, many worshipers will be oblivious to the fact that the text of a hymn or a reading occurring early in the service is related in some way to the sermon that follows half an hour later.

There are other pitfalls associated with this approach. One is the temptation to include materials primarily because they support the theme. Thus one may use an unfamiliar and unsingable hymn or a second-rate and inadequately rehearsed solo or anthem which contributes little to the worship experience but which, in academic fashion, expresses the same subject as the theme. Furthermore, another question must be considered. How does the church respond at the same time both to the narrow emphasis of a thematic service and to the wide range of needs represented by any congregation on a particular Sunday morning? For example, the theme may be "Stewardship" and every item in the service may be focused tightly on that subject. If this focus is complete, it would seem that little provision is made for the needs of a worshiper who is facing surgery, or having trouble with the kids, or coping with unemployment. Again, God *can* break through; the question is whether our liturgy tends to facilitate or to hinder this.

3. *Alternation*

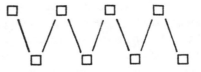

The basis of the concept of alternation is the conviction that worship is essentially an alternating series of visions of God and self. The Creator is seen and the creature responds; God calls and man answers. Much historical liturgy is organized according to this principle. The Biblical text that traditionally supports this approach is Isa. 6:1–9. This familiar passage begins with Isaiah's vision of the Lord "high and lifted up" which leads to the awareness of his own unworthiness; it concludes with God's call, "Whom shall I send?" and Isaiah's response, "Here am I! Send me."

To organize worship this way is to involve a kind of dynamic that is different from the first two. The first model depended on variety and predictability, the second on an intellectual construct. This third invokes a process that is familiar both in human experience and in Scriptural example. Isaiah's encounter with God was similar to that of Jeremiah or Moses. It was in essense a dialogue. The strength of this approach lies not so much in the visibility of its rational structure as in its intrinsic dialogical appropriateness. It "feels" right. It proceeds after the fashion of other familiar relationships, whether of person with person or of person with God. It is a natural sequence of events wherein praise is followed by self-appraisal and confession which in turn is followed by absolution and the announcing of God's forgiveness and cleansing. All of this leads appropriately to the final response to God's unconditional acceptance which generates in us the desire to do his will.

Throughout its history, much of the church's worship has followed this pattern. It would seem to be sufficient to suggest this as the ideal model when so many Christians have found it so. This would be true except for one thing. Functionally, a liturgy that is organized this way almost requires, by its very nature, the participation of a priestly figure—one who speaks to God on behalf of the people and, more importantly, one who speaks as the voice of God in asking the searching question, pronouncing the absolution, and calling to commitment. This sometimes causes a bit of uneasiness within those free-church communities which are self-consciously committed to the concept of the priesthood of *all* believers. This is not to say that an understanding of worship as *alternation* is impossible to work out in such a theological climate—only that it can be somewhat awkward and inconsistent at times. It is for this reason that a fourth model is suggested. This is one that retains the dialogical element and is rooted in the nature of the church as a community.

4. *Conversational*

The best way to describe the conversational concept is to invite you to imagine yourself as part of a small intimate group of Christians who have gathered to worship informally. Perhaps one person begins by commenting on a particular experience of awareness of God's presence and greatness and suggests the singing of "How Great Thou Art." After this is sung, another person responds by saying: "I met Bill today and we had a long conversation. I feel that he has so many problems at this time that he would have difficulty singing that song." Still another says, "Let's take a minute and pray for him," and this is done. After the prayer another suggests, "Here is a passage of Scripture that speaks to the kind of need we have just been praying about" and it is read. And so the fellowship continues. A variety of things may be experienced, but each of them will have a specific purposefulness *that grows out of the preceding event.* There is a thread of conversation, of statement and response, of question and answer that gives coherence to that which is done.

This is far different from the varied assortment of religious items that have been combined in the first model. Neither does it follow any particular theme. As one experience leads to another, a wide variety of subjects may be included. It is not self-conscious about whether the emphasis at any given moment is upon God or upon persons.

This kind of experience is a familiar one to many Christians. As described, however, it is limited to small groups, composed of persons who know one another well and who share a common level of commitment to Christianity. If any of these three elements (size, mutual awareness, common commitment) are changed substantially, the ability of the group to move extemporaneously and meaningfully is diminished. At such a point, liturgical structure may helpfully be involved.

A major function of any liturgy is to assist in overcoming the problems that are related to the three characteristics mentioned. When the congregation is large, when it is made up of persons who are strangers to one another, or when it includes persons representing a wide variety of understandings of Christianity and commitment to it, then structure for worship is usually necessary.

The *conversational* process, as described, can be used for *planning* worship. Thus, when the singing of a hymn is planned, its choice and even the determination to sing at all will be a result of the prayer or the anthem or the Scripture passage that has just preceded it. An anthem might function as an opening call to praise, as a part of the pastoral prayer, as a response to the sermon, or even in the middle of the sermon as an illustration or further exposition of some point. Its position will not be rigidly and predictably fixed within the service. Rather, it will be like all the other elements—flexible in order to best serve this conversational style. The basic difference between the order of worship as experienced by the small group or as structured for the large one is that for the first it is an extemporaneous experience. For the second, though the conversational aspect is retained, that conversation takes place between those persons who *plan* the liturgy.

If this approach is followed, it is quite possible that each week's service will be quite different from the previous one. This unpredictability will be quite unsettling for the person whose highest expectation is that worship be predictable; it will be disturbing for the worshiper who wants to remain passive and unthinking. It can be exciting and creatively provocative for that person who desires that worship be dynamic, challenging, and "real." The issue is not how we can identify and sort out persons with the first attitude but rather how we can encourage all toward the second.

Some implications about these four models are worth considering. The *variety* and the *thematic* services frequently exist in a church where worship is considered primarily as the preaching of the Word, and secondarily as engaging in other things which, though good and appropriate, are of a lesser order of value. The sermon is the focal point toward which all else moves; the gem embedded in a matrix of more ordinary substance. The function of these other things may still be considered as quite important as they provide an attractive, even inspiring experience. They may serve to reinforce both the individual's commitment to faith and the church's sense of identity. Nevertheless, their inclusion is negotiable; worship could still take place if some of them were eliminated. The sermon and the Sacraments are the essential elements.

With the concepts of *alternation* and *conversation* something quite different is happening. Underlying these concepts is the assumption that worship is intrinsically more than preaching. In fact, preaching is only one of a number of equally important and valid experiences, and worship represents the sum of them all. This is in accord with Paul as he suggests to the Corinthian church that at their meetings everyone should be ready with a psalm (song) or a sermon or a revelation, and all should be prepared to sing or pray or bless God with both the spirit and the mind (I Cor. 14:15ff.).

This distinction concerning the relative importance of the sermon may be somewhat exaggerated, but it is a real one. It will decisively affect the way one proceeds in planning a worship service.

PLANNING

Who Plans Worship?

This question must be met on two levels. The first level deals with the matter of responsibility. The common situation in many denominations is that the pastor is responsible. As mentioned in relation to the choosing of hymns, this responsibility may be formally assigned or customarily assumed. It is to be expected that the musician, also, will have specific areas of responsibility. Both the musician and the pastor must, of course, also have authority that is commensurate with the extent of responsibility.

The second level does not deal with authority but with optimum function. It has been the basic premise of all our considerations that the adequate functioning of music in a church requires a team effort. The ultimate focus of this concept is seen in the worship service.

In the *variety* model of worship, several persons provide input, but there is little or no interaction as a team. No one's thinking is affected by that of another person. With the *thematic* model, the musician must respond to an assigned theme, but there is still no essential need for interaction with the pastor.

The *alternation* service has the curious aspect of combining rigid predetermined structure (the aspect of alternation) with the possibility, almost the need, of creative flexibility. It is virtually impossible to bring this off either without having a detailed structure or without taking time for discussion between the pastor and the musician.

It is intrinsic to the *conversational* model that it must develop as the result of conversation. When such a service is planned, the central dynamic is the imagined replication of the experience of the small, intimate circle of worshipers.

It is possible for one person to imagine being in the role of each participant in the conversation and to plan the worship service accordingly. There will be many times and situations when the pastor and the musician should think this way. In fact, it should become the normal way of making choices in the planning of any kind of worship experience—not only the Sunday morning hour. However, the greatest potential value of this concept is in actually bringing together the perceptions, experiences, skills, and resources of a group of persons. There are several ways of doing this.

A commonly followed procedure is to have the planning group consist of the participants in the service. These will most likely be staff members—the pastor, the choir director, the organist, the assistant pastor, etc. The amount of time involved will be substantial. A basic question to be answered is whether the investment of time is worth the benefits derived.

A second approach would involve a lay group. This might be a worship committee that is elected for the year and that functions with the pastor and the staff to some degree in the planning of all worship services. Alternatively, they might have particular responsibility and involvement only occasionally—perhaps once or twice a month.

A third alternative would be to develop a task group for the planning of worship. Such a group would exist for a limited period and be responsible for a specified number of services. There might be some continuity of interested and experienced persons from one group to the succeeding one. The commitment, however, would always be to a limited time frame.

Fourthly, some churches have found it a stimulating and growing experience to involve the whole congregation in determining the content and style of some or all of the worship services. An invitation would be extended to any persons who are interested. They might meet over coffee after Sunday worship to consider the nature of future services. Their discussion might include such things as sermon topics or passages, assuming that a lectionary is not used; aspects of a topic or passage felt to be of particular interst or need; the type and specific content of both congregational and special music; the nature of the room in which worship takes place (assuming that variable possibilities exist); in fact, anything that has to do with the congregation at worship.

We have been somewhat reluctant to involve laity in the planning of worship. One reason has to do with the elements of responsibility and authority. For lay involvement to have significant meaning, these persons must ultimately be able to make some decisions that matter. This possibility poses a threat to many pastors, and does, indeed, have an element of risk. Part of the reason for the pastor's concern is the suspicion that these persons simply do not understand what is involved. They can't do it properly. However, if they have only minimal skill, it may be because they have not had the opportunity to learn and develop greater competence. If this is unexplored territory, some help can be found in a book on worship by Wilfred Bailey which devotes a major section to "Involvement of the Laity."[31]

It is much simpler and more efficient for the pastor and the musician to take last week's bulletin, make the appropriate changes, and pass the whole thing on to the secretary. The alternative is going to take time and energy. It will probably result in some sticky and difficult learning experiences for everyone involved. There is no point in getting into all this unless it is decided that training for worship is also an important part of "equipping the saints for the work of ministry."

How Is Worship Planned?

The individual, staff, or laity group that plans worship will first have to come to some basic conclusions. For example, what is the relationship of preaching and the Sacraments to the total worship experience? What is the unique aspect of the pastor's role in worship? What kinds of expertise need to be developed and utilized in planning and leading public worship? What is the possible range of worship styles and varieties of experiences that is appropriate for this congregation?

After these are clarified, the most critical issue is the expenditure of time. The conversational model must be re-created each week. This task can easily occupy half a day with several persons involved. For the minister who believes that true worship is the hearing of preaching and the observing of the Sacraments, this would be an inappropriate investment of time. Perhaps this is why the variety model is so ubiquitous.

A question can reasonably be raised as to whether the *variety* model achieves that which is most to be desired in worship. There is no question but that it is the quickest, easiest, most efficient way to put a service together week after week, assuming that a denominational liturgy is not followed. It demands no meeting of the participating leaders. It makes no particular requirements of advance planning for the organist or the choir director. Each individual, at his or her time and place of convenience, can make the necessary decisions. Even these decisions are simplified because they require only the choice of whatever music is best prepared and ready at the moment. The only inflexible aspect is the deadline for the specific items to be listed in the order of service. Even this can

be circumvented by the simple printing of the word "Anthem" or "Prelude" or "Special Music" without further
specifications. This is a sensible way to proceed if all
these things are simply preliminaries and the concern is
not with their interrelationship but only that each of
them be done as well as possible.

· The *thematic* type of service is slightly more demand-
ing of time required for preparation. The pastor will have
to make a long-range commitment to a series of themes.
The choosing of hymns will require the use of a topical
index. The choir director will need to search for appropriate anthems, and the scheduling of them for rehearsal
will be determined by the sequence of the pastor's
themes. The organist faces a similar requirement,
though less urgent, since specific connectives between
the themes and organ music are not as necessary. As long
as the pattern remains unchanged, there is still no inescapable need for participating worship leaders to expend
time deliberating together.

Within the *alternation* service, by definition the basic
pattern is established. It is an easy matter to assemble
hymns, readings, and prayers that express the appropriate alternation of ideas. The matter of anthem or solo is
more difficult. If the pattern of God–man–God–man–
God–man is faithfully adhered to then, provision must be
made for a variable placing of the anthem or the solo
within the service. Thus an anthem of praise or one of
confession would be placed in the appropriate part of the
worship experience. A further flexibility can be achieved
by giving particular emphasis week by week to one or
another of the steps in the sequence. Thus, one Sunday
might emphasize the aspect of praise, the vision of God,
and that section of the service might include hymn(s),

reading(s), and perhaps special music. In that service, one of the other sections, perhaps that dealing with God's absolution and acceptance, might be brief. Another Sunday the emphasis might move to another aspect of the sequence. A logical extension of these matters of variable placement and emphasis involves the sermon. The same rationale that has governed everything else suggests that it should be located within the service in a place appropriate to its content.

All of this begins to complicate things. To accept the possibility of a variable location of the anthem is to become committed to some week-by-week negotiation between the musician and the pastor. To take the further step of variable emphasis is to accept the inevitable task of spending a significant amount of time in planning. Once this degree of flexibility is present, the possibility is at hand that every service will be a new creation. Then the planners of worship are going to need to meet each week to decide just what they feel the next worship service is supposed to do and just what choice and combination of Scripture, prayer, music, preaching, etc., will best accomplish the desired end.

The *conversational* service requires a great investment of time because of the necessity for participants in the service to work together in planning it. Some items will be relatively inflexible in nature and the planning must begin with these in mind. Perhaps the anthem for the week, one of praise, is arbitrarily established as the beginning of worship. Then the question must be asked: "For what does the mood and text of the anthem prepare us? What hymn or reading or prayer or action might be a reasonable response to or continuation of it?" The question is not as in the variety service, "What comes after the anthem?" but rather "What comes after *this* anthem?" In this manner each part of the worship experience is chosen, considering both the readiness which exists for that particular expression and also the consequent response which might be made to it. One other question must be kept in mind: "How can this 'conversation' be led around to the subject of the sermon?" Once that is decided, a determination must be made as to an appropriate response by the congregation to that particular sermon. This might be the singing of a hymn, the abrupt ending of the service to send the congregation out to some kind of action, a time of reflection or of focused prayer, an opportunity for related comments by individual worshipers, a time of commitment to some task or stance or value—internalized or visibly expressed. Or perhaps there can be a combination of several of these.

Besides time, such an approach to the planning of worship requires imagination, commitment to the value of such worship, and a careful appraising of everything that is to be said, sung, or done. Attempting this would appear to be unreasonably time-consuming except for two factors.

First, after several such services have been created, certain patterns of relationships will begin to emerge. It is not imperative that each worship experience have a different structure from every other. This is not the point. Rather, it is important that the conversational flow must not be sacrificed to the maintaining of a particular structure. After a time, it will be apparent that, for instance, certain ways of beginning the service or of combining hymn or anthem or Scripture with silent or spoken prayer can be repeated. Thus, as the worship leaders begin to develop a series of models with which to work, and as they become accustomed to this way of thinking, the process is speeded up.

Second, this conversational worship is both a kind of style of functioning and a way of planning. As such, it can be usefully involved at any time, to any degree. Thus, even if the variety type of service is maintained, it can be improved by identifying and strengthening the conversational type of relationships whenever they occur. For example, if a hymn with a text which is a prayer immediately precedes the pastoral prayer, it can be helpful for the pastor to call the congregation to prayer *before* the hymn is sung, thus to identify it as part of that prayer experience. The worship leader might well pick up some of the language from the end of the hymn to begin the spoken prayer. What is involved here is partly a principle for the planning of worship and partly a suggestion for the manner of conducting it. It is a sensitivity to relationships, the ability to recognize them, and a skill in the art of helping others to be aware of them.

Such sensitivity might be illustrated thusly. One pastor might compliment the choir at the conclusion of the anthem by saying: "That was beautiful! You sang it remarkably well as you always do. We always appreciate your ministry." Another pastor might respond to the mood of the music, pick up the idea expressed, perhaps even some of the concluding text, and make this part of the following prayer or introduction to Scripture or sermon. The first has drawn attention to the choir and to its competent contribution to the variety of experiences; the second has implied that the choir has said something so important, and done it so well, that it is worth taking seriously. The latter is both the greater compliment to the choir and the better experience of worship.

If the congregation has been used to years of a-rational worship, it is not likely that its members will immediately be aware of a change if such is made. They will need help in developing new perceptions of worship and in coming to new expectations of it. It may be useful to invite their attention to the sequential purposefulness of the various acts of worship (if they actually exist). Further, the use of brief connective sentences which identify the relationships, and the repetition of words taken from one item and used at the beginning of the next, when appropriate, can encourage awareness. The transition from passive response conditioned by years of experience with the "hymn sandwich" to alert thoughtful engagement in worship may be slow and lengthy. But it is a worthy objective.

Seven

ACOUSTICS
AND WORSHIP

Do you find it more satisfying to sing in the shower at home than in church? This isn't an unlikely experience today. Frequently, congregations that move from old, rather simple buildings to new and more elegant surroundings discover that there is a different "feel" to the worship in the new building. The new church seems "terribly big" and one worshiping there often has the sense of being alone, or at least, of being too far removed from the other people.

Congregational singing feels different also. It is as if the excitement of singing familiar and beloved songs with the People of God has vanished. Instead, there is a sense of restraint. One is extremely conscious of the sound of his or her own voice and hesitates to become conspicuous by singing too freely or loudly. The new organ sounds less exciting than comparable instruments that the music committee has heard. Some feel, with the organist, that it does not have enough volume to fill the new sanctuary with sound (a blessing to that small group for whom the organ is always too loud). The choir, for some reason, is not nearly as good as it was before. It, too, is unable to produce a fortissimo when such is desired. The actual tone of the choir has suffered as the singers find themselves straining to sing louder. Individual voices with all their faults and distinctive characteristics are heard more plainly. Strangely, the choir doesn't sing nearly as much in tune as it used to. In fact, in unaccompanied passages it now may go quite noticeably flat although in the old church this was not much of a problem. The choir members say that they can't hear the organ nearly as well and that singing is more work and not nearly as much fun as it used to be.

The minister speaks distinctly enough but too softly. Although the church is of modest size, he cannot seem to make himself heard easily. It appears that it will be necessary to add a larger amplifier and more speakers to the public-address system. For his part, he senses that when he speaks, his voice "drops to the floor just on the other side of the pulpit." He feels more tired than he used to after preaching on Sunday morning. There seems to be a certain detachment or remoteness from the persons in the congregation, although he had hoped for just the opposite relationship in the new building.

Now these things could have a number of varied and unrelated causes. When they occur together it is quite likely that they are the result of the acoustical characteristics of the new building. Many congregations are discovering too late that because they gave inadequate consideration to the matter of acoustics when the new building was planned and built, they have ended up with a beautiful church in which it is difficult or impossible to do the things they desire as a basic part of Christian worship.

This contrast between an old and a new sanctuary has been drawn to identify acoustical characteristics of a live or dead room. Some of these characteristics will be present in whatever room you worship. The effects of environment are inescapable. The acoustical nature of a room will affect everything that takes place in it.

Sound Characteristics

There are a number of factors concerning the behavior of sound which affect the acoustical environment. Among these, *reverberation* is of particular importance in the situation described above. Reverberation is described acoustically as "the persistence of a sound after the generating source has ceased to function." This is not the same as *echo,* which is "the distinct reiteration of a sound." When echo is present, the initial sound is heard repeated, perhaps once, perhaps many times. Echo is *never* desirable—an appropriate amount of reverberation is. When reverberation is present, a sound (perhaps that of a loud organ chord) is heard to die away slowly. The duration of this dying away is measured as "reverberation time." The reverberation time of a large cathedral may be as much as ten to fifteen seconds; that of the hypothetical new church mentioned above might be one second or less.

There are several factors that affect reverberation. These include the volume of air enclosed within a room, the shape of that room and of the various surfaces within it, and the nature of the material of which these surfaces are made or with which they are covered. Sound waves have properties similar to those of light waves. They will be reflected by certain hard surfaces and absorbed by other soft ones, just as light is reflected by a mirror or light-colored surface and absorbed by a substance such as black velvet. Reverberation is increased when sounds are reflected; it is decreased when they are absorbed. The present-day acoustical problem in many churches centers here. When church structures were built mainly of unadorned wood, stone, or hard plaster they tended to be reverberant as these are all substances that reflect sound. The old church which was referred to probably had wooden pews sitting on a wooden floor. There may have been a runner of thin hard rubber down the aisles. The walls may have been plain hard plaster; the ceiling as well. If not, they were undoubtedly made of wood, with perhaps some large heavy folding wooden doors.

In contrast to this, today's building practice makes much use of ceiling finishes of soft, absorbent insulating material and of soft interior plaster which is blown on, serving as comparatively inexpensive final color and finish coat as well as providing some heat and sound insulation. Congregational desires will likely call for the extensive use of carpeting, drapes, and perhaps cushioned or upholstered pews. All of these substances and materials absorb sound to a large degree. The use of a combination of these things can be expected to produce a room that is acoustically dead. Such a room can cause all the problems for congregation, choir, organ, and minister that were mentioned above.

ACOUSTICS AND FUNCTION

A room that is too dead acoustically can be as unsuited for public worship as one that is too live. It is this that many committees, architects, and builders fail to recognize. In the last five decades much has been made of the problems of noise and echo in building design, but insufficient attention has been given to the fact that a room for public worship has certain unique acoustical needs. In an office, library, or restaurant it is desirable to reduce all noise as much as possible, so sound-absorbent materials are used extensively. In the theater, lecture room, or concert hall an attempt is made to reinforce sounds that come from the platform end of the room and to eliminate echo. No provision is made to encourage and strengthen sounds made by the audience. To the contrary, it is desirable to stifle any noise that might be initiated there. The rustling of programs, the sound of heels striking a hard surface on an aisle, coughing and the clearing of throats —all of this kind of sound is viewed as undesirable. In a church, however, it is essential that there be reinforcement of sounds coming from *all* parts of the room if the congregation is to participate appropriately.

The church situation is unique. It is not one that places total emphasis upon a performance by a few individuals for the sake of an audience. Rather, the audience has become a congregation—the gathered People of God who have come to join in acts of worship and edification; to "stir up one another to love and good works" and to "offer up the sweet sacrifice of praise." To recognize this as the true function of the church as it meets for worship is to affect contemporary church design. More and more buildings are being planned to emphasize the place and function of the congregation as being "gathered round" rather than merely observing. Thus the round building or something similar takes the place of the long and narrow one. It is in direct, unfortunate contradiction of this healthy architectural trend to create an acoustical situation in which each worshiper feels isolated, cut off, inhibited, restrained from taking his or her rightful place of active vocal participation in worship.

There has been a tendency to view this issue as a tension between the acoustical needs for speech as over against those for music.[32] It is true that some music can function well in a room with a reverberation period which is so long that it interferes with distinct speech (perhaps five to ten seconds). However, it does not follow that the elimination of reverberation will create a situation that is ideal for speech. Rather, such elimination will only create the need for more voice amplification (which might otherwise be unnecessary). At the same time, in such a room, the voice of the speaker loses some of its natural qualities, and the act of speaking becomes difficult and strained.

As for musical requirements, a room for worship should enhance and reinforce the musical sounds made within it the way the body or sounding box of a violin strengthens the sounds made by the vibrating strings. Music of all kinds needs some reverberation, both to strengthen its sound for the listener and to bring reassurance, support, and satisfaction to the one creating it. Concerning this, Sir James Jeans, in his book *Science and Music,* makes the following comment:

> A long period of reverberation naturally induces an exhilarating feeling of effortless power, not to mention a welcome slurring over of roughness and inequalities of force and tempo, while a short period produces the despair of ineffectual struggle. The music has only had time to show its blemishes in all their nakedness, and is already dead.[33]

In a normal church situation this need for support exists for *every* person who is participating in the worship service.

SUGGESTIONS FOR ACTION

The Present Situation

If there is a problem in the present acoustical situation, it is quite likely to be deadness—lack of enough reverberation. If such is the case, tinkering with the amplifying system will be of no significant help. The problem cannot be cured by rearranging the speakers or adding more of them. Such action may help the congregation to hear, but it fails to address the part of the problem that affects the person producing the sound—i.e., everyone in the room.

The most direct and difficult corrective will involve the removal of some of the sound-absorbent material—carpet, drapes, acoustical tile. Psychologically, this is a difficult process. The intangible acoustical gain is hard to measure over against the loss of some cherished and expensive bit of decoration. This will be true, even though the nature of worship in that room is at stake.

A less radical measure may be to paint over the soft sprayed-on acoustical plaster. Several coats of hard paint are usually necessary to get a surface that will reflect sound. This should *not* be done to the back wall of the room—that wall opposite the pulpit. Because that surface is easily a source of echo, it is frequently and appropriately made to absorb sound rather than to reflect it.

If none of the above steps is possible, at least an awareness of the problem will dictate some consideration of the way the room is used. It will be important to get all persons in the room as close together as possible. Hymns will need to be sung at a faster tempo than if the room were reverberant. Explore the possibility of moving musical events, such as choir programs, congregational hymn sings, to another room if one is available.

If the present room is too live, remedial procedures are much easier. They involve simply introducing sound-absorbent materials, possibly in small amounts. These materials can be in the form of carpet, hangings, banners, decorative panels of acoustical tile. These are all things that can be experimented with and easily applied, either temporarily or permanently.

The Changing Situation

Frequently, when a church is built, for financial reasons the congregation sets as a future goal the addition of some decorative elements such as carpet or drapes. Or the possibility of adding them will appear when redecorating an older building. At such a time, the persons concerned with the music and worship of the church should press for a serious consideration of alternatives. Are drapes behind the choir worth the loss of enjoyable and competent singing? Is the increased visual and tactile pleasure of new carpet in the church worth the loss in involvement and sense of interrelationship on the part of the congregation?

One of the ways to measure this is to look in your community for other church buildings that have a variety of acoustical characteristics. On one day, take a representative group from your congregation and visit these rooms in quick succession. Experience what it means to talk, sing, and read in a variety of acoustical environments. Hear the sound of musical instruments in each. You may even be able to find a series of differing environments in your own church—a hallway that is live; a comfortably furnished parlor that is dead. You can get the equivalent of an acoustically dead room by going outdoors and standing on grass to sing and listen.

The New Situation

The procedures suggested in "The Changing Situation" are all relevant for a church that is planning a new building. Other considerations will also be involved. The matter of reverberation will be affected by the basic design of the room—its shape. It is necessary to take into account the control of background noise (heating, air conditioning), sound insulation (the elimination of unwanted noise from outside traffic or other church activities going on at the same time as worship), and the avoidance of "dead spots" (the undesired focus of sounds in some areas of the room with corresponding loss in others —a matter of design).

Because the problems involved are complex, the advice of a specialist in *church* acoustics should be sought as a part of the process of designing and building a new structure. This should not be considered a luxury, but rather a reasonable recognition that the whole experience of the congregation in using the new building is at stake. If no church-oriented acoustical engineer is available, then be sure that the architect *and* the builder understand the issues that have been raised. Make these a matter of discussion and investigation.

ACOUSTICAL NEEDS

The specific acoustical needs for all members of a worshiping community would include the following:

Preacher—needs to be able to talk easily, naturally, with the assurance of being heard. Hard surfaces above, behind, and beneath the preacher will tend to facilitate this; soft absorbent ones will hinder it. The acoustical nature of the whole room will be the primary determining factor.

Choir—needs effortless ease in singing and the consequent lack of inhibition. In addition, the members need to be able to hear one another, thus making it possible to sing in tune and with unity. It is extremely dysfunctional to carpet the area where they sing or to have drapery beside or behind them. As little as one narrow panel of drapery behind the choir can be enough to alter significantly the acoustical characteristics of the chancel.

Organ—needs sufficient reverberation to "soften," blend, enhance, and reinforce the tone. In addition, it is important that the sound spread evenly throughout the room with minimal emphasis on the location of its source. The congregation, choir, and organist should all hear the organ with equal loudness and clarity. This will be partially a matter of location and partially a matter of acoustics.

Congregation—needs clear and easy hearing of speech and music. This means that these sounds must be both loud enough and intelligible—that is, undisturbed by echo or excess reverberation. Also, the congregation needs uninhibited freedom to speak or sing. This will be related to the presence of an acoustical environment that communicates a feeling of togetherness. Ideally, the room should be such that a handful of people scattered throughout it could converse easily and naturally with one another.

Upholstered pews are absorbent, but this is not necessarily dysfunctional in reducing desired reverberation. People are also absorbent. Upholstered pews will simply give the room the same acoustical characteristics whether it is occupied or empty. With hard pews or chairs, the room will be more reverberant when empty than when people are present. This can be quite disconcerting to the choir that rehearses in the empty room, gaining support from its reverberation, and attempts to minister in a room that has suddenly become acoustically dead because of the presence of the congregation.

A pastor or a committee should take the following things into account in any action involving the new construction, remodeling, or decorating of a room for worship:

1. The church has a unique purpose in meeting together—one that differs from other kinds of gatherings and one that places emphasis on individual participation.

2. Preaching, organ music, choral music, congregational singing, and speaking are all drastically affected for good or ill by the acoustical environment in which they take place.

3. Acoustical requirements for speech and music may differ to some degree but are not necessarily contradictory.

4. It is easier to deaden a room after it is built and tested than it is to make it more alive. There are a number of ways in which sound-absorbent materials can be added easily to hard surfaces. The opposite, the hardening of soft surfaces, is more difficult and expensive.

5. Reverberation time cannot be effectively altered by any use of electronic amplification. That process is an important consideration, but it deals with other hearing needs.

6. The matter of reverberation, which has been the focus of attention in this chapter, is the acoustical issue most likely to affect the use of music in worship. It is also the most ignored or misunderstood.

When a church redecorates or builds, it may find itself changing its whole experience of public worship for reasons that are neither theological nor liturgical. Such changes may not be willfully sought but forced upon it by an unplanned acoustical situation. People sing in the shower because it is acoustically satisfying. On the other hand, they keep quiet in the "slumber room" of a mortuary. One reason for this is that such a room is constructed and decorated and acoustically treated in such a manner as to induce silence. We would do well to avoid turning our church sanctuaries into slumber rooms.

Eight

AGE OF ROCK
OR ROCK OF AGES?

In the past two decades there has been a revolution in church music. It is important that the minister and the musician understand the nature of this upheaval and its consequent implications for present and future ministry. Perhaps the most dramatic aspect of this revolution is that pop music has invaded the church. This invasion is not the totality of the revolution, but it serves as a symbol of what has been happening and is worthy of our consideration.

THE SITUATION AT MID-CENTURY

At the middle of the twentieth century the distinction between pop (or secular) music and church (or sacred) music was clearly established. (I am using the term "pop" to refer to any musical idiom that is part of the light, commercial entertainment scene.) Each had its own territory which was clearly defined and clearly separate from the other.

Outside the Church

For generations, pop music existed as a symbol of cultural evil. It was assumed that neither a cultured person nor one seriously committed to the Christian faith would have anything to do with ragtime, jazz, swing, or rock. Certainly it was unthinkable that these profane sounds could be used appropriately in Christian worship. Rather, they were characterized by such terms as inappropriate, disrespectful, irreverent, profane, sinful, diabolical. No doubt, part of the reason for this long-standing attitude lay in the association of these musical sounds with certain kinds of places and activities that were, themselves, expected to be rejected by both the Christian and the cultured person.

However, with the development of communication by the middle of the twentieth century, this whole phenomenon of equating place and sound was altered. For instance, with the emergence of radio, the phonograph, television, and the tape cassette, jazz no longer existed only in the bordello of New Orleans or the speakeasy of Chicago. It had found its way into the deacon's living room or, at least, into the bedroom of his son or daughter. In many forms, pop music had been insidiously emerging from the dark places where it lurked at the beginning of the century and had penetrated virtually all of society.

A similar phenomenon existed for many generations on the foreign mission field. Consistently around the world, missionaries had taught that when the Christian faith was embraced, it was necessary for the convert to learn a new kind of music in order to express the new-found faith. The sound of the drums (that is, the sound of colloquial or pop music) was identified as the sound of the old pagan life; the new life in Christ had to be expressed in a new kind of music (the music of Western European and American Christendom).

Forces were at work by mid-century to bring this practice into question. Of primary importance among these was the rising pressure of nationalism. The assumption that "Western was better and more Christian" was rejected. As a great deal of leadership was transferred from Western missionaries to indigenous personnel, so the appropriateness of indigenous musical expression was reexamined and affirmed.

Within the Church

Normally at mid-century, any serious student of church music was taught that appropriate music for the church's use should be both *good* ("only the best is adequate for the service of God") and *sacred* (that is, avoiding any secular connotations).

Remember the comment by Archibald Davison, quoted in Chapter 5, to the effect that church music should sound like "a speech apart; remote, archaic perhaps, sacerdotal, strange; a language to which the church alone would be hospitable." This was not a remarkable attitude but was typical of church music leaders. Earlier in the twentieth century we find other similar comments.

> And if we consider and ask ourselves what sort of music we should wish to hear on entering church, we should surely, in describing our ideal, say first of all that it must be something different from what is heard elsewhere; that it must be a sacred music.[34]

That statement was made by Robert Bridges, poet laureate of England. The following comment was by R. G. McCutchan, noted American Methodist church musician and hymnologist:

> Church music should be different from popular, social music. There should be a definite association of music used in our churches with spiritual things.[35]

And in the words of a pastor early in the twentieth century:

> The music of the Church must ever be apart from that of the world. All trivial music should be discarded and only such modern music as is written in an Ecclesiastical style, and can be shown to be the work of men in communion with the Church should be allowed a place in the Church's song.[36]

While some church musicians would view these statements as rather extreme, there is no question but that the whole church self-consciously suspected or avoided any musical idiom that might be mistaken for a secular one. A particular church might express itself musically through Gregorian chant, psalm tunes, Victorian hymnody, gospel songs, or evangelistic choruses from the 1930's, but none of these could ever be mistakenly confused with any pop idiom of the day. A kind of "evangelical pop" existed, starting perhaps with the work of Ralph Carmichael in the late 1940's, which used a variety of instruments and choral techniques closely related to secular groups of the time such as Fred Waring and his Pennsylvanians. Even this, however, which became the staple fare of many Christian radio stations, had a distinctive religious quality that immediately identified it for what it was and distinguished it from the secular music of the same period. The church choir might be singing Palestrina, Bach, Stainer, Harry Rowe Shelley, T. Tertius Noble, or John Peterson, but none of their anthems would be confused with the music of the everyday world.

THE REVOLUTION

Pop Music Invades the Church

About 1960 all of this began to change. The most noteworthy initial impetus came from Geoffrey Beaumont's *20th Century Folk Mass,* which was released in England late in the 1950's. This quickly crossed the ocean and received attention in this country as the "Jazz Mass" (although the musical idiom used was that of swing of the late 1930's). Within the next decade there emerged explosively an incredible variety of ventures in the experimental use of various pop idioms for the purpose of worship and evangelism.[37] These ventures included as many kinds of pop sounds as can be identified across the spectrum of varieties of entertainment music. Furthermore, such experiments were carried on by virtually all segments of the church (excepting only Eastern Orthodoxy). Catholic and Protestant, American and European, liturgical and free churches, liberal and conservative, urban and rural, cathedral and storefront—all of these participated. This is not to say that every congregation was involved, but rather, that representative groups from all conceivable forms of the church were found exploring these new possibilities. In the mid-1960's particular impetus came from two directions. Evangelical Protestantism was greatly influenced by the Billy Graham films and the use they made of pop sounds (though very little of this new sound found its way into the Graham meetings themselves). Roman Catholicism was affected by the determinations of the Second Vatican Council among which were two matters of particular relevance here: (1) that around the world the liturgy was to use the vernacular language rather than the traditional Latin and (2) that congregational music in the vernacular was to be encouraged.

On the foreign mission field at this same time forces combined to encourage the use of hitherto rejected colloquial native musical idioms. (This is, of course, the same issue as that of whether colloquial secular music should be used in this country.) The emerging attitude is reflected in the record jacket notes of Father Hazen's *Missa Luba* (created in the Congo about the same time as Father Beaumont's *Folk Mass* was being composed in England). One reads concerning his attitude: "I honor your ways and those of your fathers. If you learn this Christian mass, please sing it in the manner of your people, not in my way but in your way."

The Church Invades Pop Music

During this same period, the field of pop music was affected as dramatically as that of church music. Starting in the 1950's, folk musicians such as Bob Dylan began to write and sing songs that, while not overtly religious, were focused on various moral issues—the kind of issues with which the church appropriately should be concerned. Soon songs began to appear that were based on expressions or passages of Scripture—for example, "Turn, Turn, Turn," or Leonard Cohen's "Story of Isaac." This was followed by the rising to popularity of specific hymn materials such as the Hawkins Singers' "O Happy Day" or Judy Collins' "Amazing Grace." Finally, such overtly Christian things as *Godspell, Jesus Christ Superstar,* and Leonard Bernstein's *Mass* began to be created for and find acceptance in society completely outside the church. Thus, the categories of sacred and secular, each of which had been so impervious to the other in 1950, had penetrated each other in a substantial way by 1975.

Implications of the Revolution

Affirmation of the Contemporary

Hitherto, very little music that used contemporary idioms of any kind was available to the average church musician. A sophisticated and professionally competent choirmaster could use Benjamin Britten or Daniel Pinkham to express this element of contemporaneity. However, virtually no such music was available that was capable of being performed by the average volunteer choir possessing modest musical resources. Twentieth-century hymns written in traditional style but using contemporary language and imagery were remarkably rare. However, with this new music, for the first time in the twentieth century the ordinary church musician found it possible to say through music, "Jesus Christ is our contemporary."

Affirmation of the Colloquial

An even greater contribution to the church was the recovery of the value, even the need, of the colloquial. At mid-century both musical and poetic standards for the writing of new church music were unreasonably high. (This was true in spite of the enormous quantity of second-rate commercially inspired music.) Hymnological criteria were derived, for example, from such excellent hymns as Charles Wesley's "Christ the Lord Is Risen Today" or "Hark! the Herald Angels Sing." It was forgotten that these were not typical; that only a handful (a little over two hundred) of the more than six thousand hymns written by him persist into this century. Most were discarded long ago as having little value. Nevertheless, the contemporary writer of new hymns was compelled to measure the worth of his creation by the very best—the distillate of Watts or Wesley. This was, of course, unreasonable and enormously inhibiting. With the emerging acceptance of the colloquial, often in the form of folk music, we rediscovered the concept of "disposable music." This discovery brought with it a willingness to encourage creativity no matter what the level of sophistication of the creation.

By accepting the colloquial, the church was saying two things. First, it was willing to clothe the great truths of the Christian faith in forms with which the most unsophisticated could identify and in which such persons could participate. In other words, this became the embodying of I Cor. 1:2, where the apostle Paul suggests that even that which is foolish, low, or despised may communicate the truth of the gospel as well as or better than that which is eloquent, wise, and clever. Second, it was not necessary to learn a special "religious" musical language to sing about the faith. This is somewhat similar to the issues of whether worship demands a special kind of architecture (perhaps Gothic or radical contemporary), of clothing (ecclesiastical garments or Sunday finery of middle-class suburbia), or of language (Latin or Elizabethan English). By 1970 much of the church was saying in effect, "We are willing to talk (sing) to you in your language without requiring that you learn ours first."

There are important precedents for such an attitude on the part of the church regarding its music. The music of the gospel songs, one of the most cherished forms of "special" religious musical expression today, was the idiom of parlor music—secular music of a century ago. This idiom was used by Dwight L. Moody and Ira Sankey and other nineteenth-century evangelists precisely because it was a sound that was familiar to and accepted by the unchurched. More than a century earlier, the great revival that became Methodism moved on the singing nurtured by the Wesleys. The tunes of their new mid-eighteenth-century hymnody included the idioms of English folk music and the musical expression of the London street songs of the day. And, of course, the sixteenth-century Protestant Reformation flourished on the new music which was far more like the world outside the church than the familiar sounds which traditionally accompanied the Mass. Martin Luther's tunes would have been shockingly reminiscent of the tavern to those who had heard only Gregorian chant or polyphonic choral music in worship. Clément Marot brought his metrical psalms from French court entertainments where they had been set to popular airs to be sung by the Calvinists of Strassburg and Geneva.[38] (And they were referred to by the first Queen Elizabeth of England as "Geneva Jigs.") In the low countries the term *souterliedekens* served to identify the new vernacular rhymed versions of the psalms which were set to popular folk melodies of the

period. At the same time, up in Scotland, the Wedder-
burn brothers were becoming known through their *Gude
and Godlie Ballatis,* which were, essentially, folk ballads
about love or hunting in which a few words were changed
in order to give the song a Christian meaning. In the
Middle Ages the *lauda* existed as nonliturgical folk-
related musical expressions used by traveling evangelists
(the Franciscans). Even earlier, the metrical hymns of
Ambrose of Milan, the father of metrical hymnody, were
developed in the fourth century in the form of street
songs and work songs and marching songs of the common people.

Throughout its history, at reoccurring intervals, the
church in its music has moved to reestablish contact
with the world around it—not the sophisticated world
of the professional musician but that of the common
person. We have witnessed such a happening during
the past twenty years.

Reexamination

One additional aspect of this musical revolution has
been the pressure it has exerted on the church to reexamine certain assumptions about the nature of its faith.
Certainly it has called for the issue of sacred vs. secular
to be dealt with. Assumptions as to the existence of such
a thing as "sacred" music and as to the way such music
might be identified have been called into question.

Those who have felt that there are certain kinds of
melody or rhythm or harmony that are intrinsically
"Christian" have found difficulty, when pressed, in determining criteria. Certainly the Scriptures offer nothing
specific at this point; they simply do not deal with the

subject. Upon recognition of this fact, ground of argument often shifts to the area of "association." Certainly within a limited time frame the factor of association is an obvious and important one. However, after a bit more careful examination, another aspect emerges—simply that associational meanings can be changed. This may happen, for instance, when a pop song is used as the focus of discussion within a youth group; when a purely secular song provides the stimulus for consideration of some aspect of the gospel which it may (in nontheological terms) either affirm or contradict. For anyone who has participated in such a discussion, the future hearing of that song may call to mind associations that are very much Christian in nature. In a different way, history clearly demonstrates how music that was once identified as "secular" has become "sacred" by virtue of its use by the church.

Other matters that go far beyond music itself are also involved. The use of such pop or secular music raises a question concerning such practice in the light of the New Testament admonition to be careful to avoid conforming to the world (e.g., Rom. 12:2). Music has frequently been identified as illustrative of such conformity or lack of it. The musical issue may well prod the church to discover a deeper, more mature level of understanding of such Biblical teaching: one in which emphasis shifts from simple outward manifestations such as music, clothing, recreation, or diet to inward matters such as attitudes, priorities, goals, and commitments.

CONSEQUENCES OF THE REVOLUTION

A New Hymnody

Twenty years ago there was much lamenting on the part of church musicians that there was no twentieth-century hymnody. At least, in quantity and quality the contributions of this century fell far behind previous ones. That has changed. An enormous number of new songs for the church have appeared. The quantity is so great that there is need to emphasize the element of "disposability." Even as the situation has encouraged many persons to attempt writing texts and music, there has developed a consequent need for pastor and church musician to discriminate in the selection of such material. It may be commendable and valuable that so many have attempted to express themselves creatively in the form of a new song. The doing of this is to be encouraged and affirmed. However, most such creations will have very little persisting value. It is possible to encourage the writing and the short-lived usefulness of such songs without becoming captive to their continuing use over an extended period of time. Meanwhile, out of this mass of songs are emerging hymns that speak of the contemporaneity of the gospel as it has meaning in today's situations (for example, space travel, environmental responsibility, ecumenism). Such hymns also speak with language and images appropriate for the latter part of the twentieth century.

A New Conservatism

It is the nature of the church to be conservative. After all, its central task is to preserve the gospel so that it may be communicated to each new generation. However, this process of conservatism works in strange fashion to cause the meanings of things to change. For example, one controversy of the Reformation had to do with the elaborate ecclesiastical garments worn by the Roman Catholic priests. In reaction to this practice, some leaders made a point of wearing their nonecclesiastical working clothes while preaching. John Calvin and John Knox were two such leaders. They were university lecturers, and their working garb consisted of black robe with white tabs, and this they wore in the pulpit. Through the process of conservatism, these which were once the very symbol of objection to the wearing of special garments by the minister have become special garments for ministerial use. In similar fashion, the gospel song which used the musical style of pop music of the 1870's is now one of the musical sounds that expresses the distinctive "otherness" of the church. It did not change to take on this characteristic; it simply remained the same while other musical styles developed in society.

Today the same process is beginning to be visible. Whatever the idiom (progressive jazz, blues, ragtime, rock, etc.), the musical expressions at the beginning of this revolution all shared one common characteristic— they could *not* be identified as coming from within the church. It was intrinsic to the process that there was a combining of sacred words and truly secular music. An important part of the dynamic in operation was the fact that the church was speaking with a nonsacred kind of

music. Through the conserving process, a gap is beginning to develop between church pop and the sounds that
are emerging as new kinds of entertainment music today.
A typical "rock" musical sung by a youth choir is clearly
identifiable for what it is—a special kind of church music.
This is not necessarily bad. To raise the issue is not to
suggest that such music should be abandoned. It is,
rather, to remind ourselves of some other values which
may be desirable but which may be in danger of being
lost. It is already apparent that the "new" music of the
church and that of society's pop are developing along
diverging courses. It may be necessary to wait again for
a century until church music gets completely out of touch
with the music of society and another revolution takes
place. However, perhaps recognition of this as a continuing need in church-society relationships can encourage
some leaders in church music to seek a continually
changing response.

Commercialism

In his preface to the Weiss hymnal of 1528, Martin
Luther complained about those printers who carelessly
reprinted his hymns in their attempt to cash in on the
tremendous market that had developed for them. He
feared that his hymnbook would "be corrupted and adul-
terated by blunderheads until the good in it will be lost
and only the bad remain."[39] As happens so often in the
church, this problem is a persistent one.

The gospel song movement whose beginnings
focused in America in the 1870's provides an excellent
example of the possibilities of commercial exploitation.

In his book *Three Centuries of American Hymnody*, Henry Wilder Foote commented:

> It is said that fifty million copies of Sankey's books were sold. The publisher's profits were enormous and led to an unedifying scramble to occupy the field, though the evangelists themselves kept honorably clean of commercialism. Many hundred rival publications were issued, cheap in form and ephemeral in content.[40]

The incredible popularity of these gospel songs attracted hundreds of writers who produced thousands of different books which were sold in quantities numbering in the millions. Schools and churches were paid for out of some of these profits, and private fortunes were made by the sale of songbooks. As this mass of material grew, the number of second-rate commercially inspired songs increased with enormous rapidity. Often these were not creative expressions of faith but were instead simply response to the demand to publish another book—perhaps number six or ten in a series. In addition to their dubious origin and shoddy nature, these songs presented an additional problem by virtue of being reproduced, not by mimeograph, but within hardback covers of a songbook. The disposable possibilities had been minimized or eliminated. The result was to encourage the persistence in the church of a great number of mediocre songs. Their very existence in such numbers made it difficult to find and recognize the best of the gospel songs.

A similar process has now begun with the materials of the mid-twentieth-century musical revolution. The initial ventures in the late 1950's and the early 1960's were carried out by persons deeply committed to the issue itself. There was a kind of missionary zeal to help the church find its way into this new kind of expression and self-understanding. The first songbooks and records represented the accumulation of the best materials created and gathered by persons whose primary commitment was to ministry rather than to the carrying on of a money-making operation. By the mid-1970's, the commercial possibilities of such music have started in motion a different process. Familiar "stars" are encouraged continually to produce new records, songbooks, and musicals. Unfortunately, frequently these do not represent worthwhile new creations but are rather simply the rehashing of what has gone before. Even worse, the commercial possibilities have attracted great numbers of imitators with little capability of offering anything new or worthwhile to the church. Most reprehensible are those publishers who have simply taken the songs of a generation or two ago and dressed them up in a new contemporary-looking cover, thus attempting to suggest that they, too, are part of this movement. The result is visible in any Christian bookstore where racks are bulging with a confusing multitude of songbooks, sheet music, and records.

Pluralism

The New Testament speaks about becoming "all things to all men" (I Cor. 9:22); about how, within the gospel there cannot be "Greek and Jew, circumcised and uncircumcised, barbarian, Scythian, slave, free man" (Col. 3:11). Within the Kingdom, such distinctions are inappropriate. In the field of church music, it is consistent with such teaching to suggest that the church should not be segregated in terms of those who like and will accept only Bach or the gospel song or the old psalm tunes or Christian pop. Hitherto, we have easily accepted such segregation even as, previously, we have been willing to accept segregation on the basis of race or education or economic position. The emotionally loaded intrusion of pop has forced us to reconsider the question of whether the music of a particular church should reflect *only* the tastes of the pastor or the musician or the power group within the laity. C. S. Lewis addressed himself provocatively to this issue. He suggested that the truly "Christian" aspect of church music is present in that situation in which each is willing to subordinate his or her own tastes and desires to those of others within the community.[41] The functional result of such an attitude within the church is that one may then expect to find a variety of kinds of musical expressions and a growing appreciation of all of them.

Another way of viewing this pluralism is indicated by Jesus' teaching (Matt. 13:52) that the wise teacher is one who makes use of that which is old and that which is new. The church, with its native conservatism, will easily retain the use of that which is old (although it may need help and encouragement in distinguishing between that which is simply archaic and that which is timeless). The acceptance of the new comes with a bit more difficulty. Long before Jesus, the psalmist reminded God's people of the need to include also that which is new—the "new song" (Ps. 33:3; 96:1; 98:1; 144:9). The reasonable pragmatic wisdom is that both the old and the new have distinctive values; each can do something that the other cannot do. Therefore, both are needed for a full ministry.

The old is, first of all, the record of the church's life and faith and is in a real sense the church's memory. As such, it is important to us today. Our own sense of identity is dependent upon knowing whence we have come. There is no other way of fully knowing who we are.

Helmut Thielicke describes a postwar incident involving old (and second-rate) hymns, refugees, and theological students. The students were to accompany him to a refugee camp for a visit. He was anxious because he knew the kind of songs these refugees would be singing and knew that for the theological students they represented a kind of expression that would be scorned. However, when in the situation itself, he discovered that the students participated wholeheartedly. The old discredited songs had been invested with a kind of integrity by the lives and suffering and faith of those refugees. He spoke of how much it mattered that

> people have been comforted by these hymns, that they have died with these words on their lips, and that they learned to love these verses in the hardest hours of their lives.[42]

This is an important element in the life of the individual Christian and in the life and music of the church. One of the purposes of including this story is to illustrate that the "old" has a variety of values, all of which require recognition.

The new is needed to express the contemporaneity of the gospel—the fact that Christ lives today and that his purposes find meaning only in the reality of today's world. Beyond this, the new has the potential capability of prodding awake. *It* can energize appropriate response to the prophet Amos' declaration, "Woe to those who are at ease in Zion" (Amos 6:1). It is of the essence of the new to make uncomfortable, to stir up, to rebuke and challenge old, comfortable, and thoughtless ways of perceiving and responding. Moreover, it is only the new that can communicate with the society in which we live—that society which has not already responded to the God of the living church. Only the new can tell these people in their own language that God knows them and loves them and invites them into relationship with himself and his people.

JOINING THE REVOLUTION

This contemporary revolution in church music has aspects that are valuable and appropriate for every church. It may be easier to recognize these values then actually to make this new music a part of the worship life of the congregation. To do this involves specific matters of choice and use.

Choice

Earlier it was suggested that particular discrimination is necessary in selecting contemporary materials. As with other kinds of choral and congregational music, the easiest place to begin to evaluate is with the text. Whatever the song says should be theologically sound and useful. This criterion has two areas of application. The first, obviously, is the individual piece of music. The second is not quite so apparent. It has to do with the total body of music that is experienced by a particular church. Enticed by a pleasant musical idiom, a congregation may find itself singing and hearing contemporary music with a very limited range of theological expression. The reason for this possibility lies in a curious developmental trend in this new music.

There has been a shift of emphasis and value in the kind of texts that have been part of the revolution in church music. The original ventures took place almost entirely within the liturgical segment of the church. It was the Roman Catholics, Anglicans, Episcopalians, and Lutherans who were the innovators. The texts they used were the ones that were a familiar part of their regular worship. These tended to be traditional statements which focused on the praise of God and the reiteration of basic matters of belief. Many of them were passages from Scripture. Others came from the historical liturgies of the church, including expressions such as the Sanctus ("Holy, Holy, Holy, Lord God of Hosts"), the Agnus Dei ("O Lamb of God, that takest away the sins of the world, have mercy upon us"), and the creeds. Many traditional hymn texts were also used in contemporary music settings.

As the free church got involved in the mid-1960's, the main creative interest was shown by those identified as evangelicals. Within their circle of use, the focus shifted from the Biblical, liturgical, and hymnological expressions to the area of personal testimony and invitation. Typical of this kind of testimony is Ralph Carmichael's song "He's Everything to Me." In essence, this became a contemporary manifestation of the objectives of the gospel song of a century earlier. Today, the great majority of available music in contemporary pop idiom has texts that focus on personal salvation and witness. As with the gospel song, it is appropriate for the church to have this as a part of its message. It is inappropriate for this important expression of the faith to exclude everything else.

As discussed earlier, one aspect of this revolution has

been the encouraging of the creation of music by anyone. Much of this needs to be in the form of short-lived, "disposable" music. It is important to distinguish between this and other things which in form and cost are intended for long-term use. This movement affirms the creative possibilities of everyone. One doesn't need to be a professional musician, poet, or theologian to take guitar in hand and create something. This is good! Such songs, however, are not likely to become part of the timeless, universal musical expression of the church. Their greatest value may well be that they were written, and were an expression of a particular group at a particular time.

Be slow to buy. Take advantage of the contemporary screening process. All the material written even by the best-known and most popular composers will not be of equally high quality. This is intrinsic to the creative process. Charles Wesley wrote thousands of hymns to produce a few hundred that were truly great. This has implications for the purchase of a contemporary songbook for the congregation. A collection of songs by one individual is likely to have the largest percentage of unusable material. Only slightly better will be a collection whose copyrights are all held by one publisher. Look for books that have brought together a number of composers and copyright holders. This means that an attempt has been made to screen out all but the best and most useful songs.

In examining a hard-cover hymnal that combines contemporary and traditional songs, check the number of in-house copyrights (copyrights held by the publisher of that particular book). If this is limited to from 5 to 10 percent, there is reasonable assurance that a serious effort has been made to make available the best possible selection. If that percentage is higher, it is likely that many of those songs are included simply because they are already owned by the publisher.

Use

The First Step. Care needs to be taken in introducing a new idiom into the church's worship. Make a special effort to choose music that offers a particularly apt combination of tune and text. The new music should be an obviously fitting expression of the idea involved.

Take time to explain the reasons for what is being done. Suggest why this new idiom is appropriate for worship. This can be done just before it is sung, or at the beginning of the service. An explanatory paragraph in the bulletin can also help. The identifying of historical parallels can be particularly useful in gaining acceptance for the new. Emotional resistance may be lowered with the realization that "Blessed Assurance, Jesus Is Mine" and "A Mighty Fortress Is Our God" both used musical idioms perceived by the church of their day as secular.

Prepare a context for the new music. Don't simply replace a predictable hymn or anthem with one in a startling new idiom. Perhaps Scripture referring to the aspect of "newness" can be introduced. The context may include explanation as mentioned above. The new music might be related to a sermon that deals with newness itself, or with some aspects of the incarnation which were particularly new and disconcerting. Or the theme of the new song may be particularly pertinent to the sermon theme of the morning. In some way, let there be an obvious appropriate rationale for this new experience.

Be sure that the new music is well done. If it offends,

don't let the offense be because it was ineptly rendered, inadequately rehearsed, or beyond the capabilities of those performing it. If it involves the congregation, by all means arrange for a congregational rehearsal before the moment of using it in worship.

If the contemporary music is in the form of a congregational song, make sure that the other hymns are comfortable, familiar ones. (This will be equally true if the "new" hymn is in traditional rather than contemporary idiom.) Try to plan so that there is a reasonable expectation that the congregation will have a good singing experience somewhere in that service.

Pain of Change. Change is usually accompanied by a bit of discomfort or pain. This is especially true if the change has to do with matters of faith and worship. Furthermore, music operates in the territories of both the cognitive and the emotional. Thus, when the change experience also involves music, the discomfort is likely to be increased because of the emotional factor. Some examples from the history of classical music can illustrate this. Nicolas Slonimsky has compiled an anthology of evaluations of contemporary music of various periods by critics of the day.[43] The following quotations are from that source and show the difficulties experienced, even by professional music critics, in encountering music that was unfamiliar.

Beethoven—"Most of what he produces is so impenetrably obscure in design and so full of unaccountable and often repulsive harmonies, that he puzzles the critic as much as he perplexes the performer." (London, 1824.)

Beethoven—"We can sincerely say that rather than study this last work for beauties which do not exist, we

had far rather hear the others where beauties are plain."
(Boston, 1853, speaking of the Ninth Symphony.)

Beethoven—"Beethoven always sounds to me like the
upsetting of bags of nails with here and there an also
dropped hammer." (John Ruskin, 1881.)

Chopin—"Cunning must be the connoisseur, indeed,
who, while listening to his music can form the slightest
idea when wrong notes are being played." (London,
1845.)

Wagner—"I believe that I could write tomorrow
something similar, inspired by my cat walking down the
keyboard of the piano." (Paris, 1861, on *Tannhäuser*.)

Wagner—"I do not believe that a single composition
of Wagner will survive him." (Leipzig, 1871.)

Debussy—"Debussy's 'Afternoon of a Faun' was a
strong example of modern Ugliness." (Boston, 1904.)

Expect, then, that this new music may generate real
resistance on the part of some and ambivalance in quite
a few. Many persons will find it difficult to decide just
what to do with these brash, unaccustomed sounds in
worship. I recall a Sunday evening discussion group,
considering the subject of "Pop Music and the Church."
Conspicuously visible was a man of formidable appearance, obviously part of the power structure of that particular church. He was in his sixties, tall, thin, bald, dressed
in black suit and white shirt. He sat stiff and straight and
listened to the musical examples with a frown on his face.
During a particular bit of jazz that combined a religious
text with a strong beat, he began to relax. His foot tapped
and his whole body moved slightly with the music. Then
he shook his head vigorously back and forth, drew himself up stiffly, and the frown returned. In a few moments,
the music would get to him and the whole cycle would

begin again. He was enjoying music and responding to it; at the same time, he felt that somehow there must be something wrong with such enjoyment—especially in relationship to Christian things. Some people will not know what to do with the new experiences into which this music can lead them.

This uneasiness will be minimized if the new music is carefully chosen and sensitively introduced. Such an event can provide the occasion to reexamine basic assumptions as to what might make music sacred or profane, right or wrong for the church. It will be useful if you can offer reassurance that these new ventures are compatible with Scriptural teaching, theological belief, and the church's history. As considered under "Pluralism," this experience can also be the opportunity for discussing the impropriety of equating "I don't like this" with "This is wrong to do."

Separate but Equal. Many churches have developed a pattern of having multiple services, each with its own distinctive style. This makes a great deal of sense. Whether one's preferences are in the area of pop music with colloquial language or traditional materials, it is reasonable to prefer worship experiences that correspond to such desires. However, such a pattern of worship can also be detrimental to the process of Christian growth if it simply confirms existing preferences and expectations in the worshiper. To work against this dysfunctional aspect, it is important that those persons whose affections are attached to one style also are continuously aware of other styles and exposed to them. Both the contemporary and the traditional approaches to worship should be represented in the worship service.

Each service should accommodate to the preferences of its constituency but should not simply confirm them. The traditionalist *needs* to hear the contemporary, and the jazz devotee needs to learn from the historical.

Old Problems. While this revolution in church music has made available exciting and welcome new sounds, one must realize that contemporary music does not provide the answer to all musical problems. Some of these may simply reappear in a new guise.

Perhaps there has been difficulty with an elderly organist whose reactions are slow and whose tempos are dragging. There will be no significant gain if this person is replaced by a high school guitarist who is able to play in only one key and whose sense of rhythm is nonexistent.

Perhaps congregational singing has been poor because the acoustical nature of the room stifles the making of any sounds. Then simply changing from old to new instruments or music will not significantly improve things.

Perhaps the problem has been an undue commitment to or appetite for only one kind of music on the part of the choir, the musician, the pastor, or the congregation. If everything has been "painted in one color" musically, a problem still remains if embracing new music simply means substituting another color. Many churches that were most resistant to these new sounds a decade ago have changed over and become totally captive to them today.

Perhaps singing has been poor because in reality the people do not feel anything about their faith to motivate them to sing. Again, new music is no substitute for a vital

Christian faith; it cannot by itself create the kind of community in which persons want to share with one another in singing. It *can*, however, bring an aspect of newness that may provide the occasion for a fresh look at the nature of the gospel and the church and for a new level of commitment to them.

"Sic Transit Gloria Mundi." The traveling youth choir has been a phenomenon of the American church scene during the last decade. The very presence of one has almost become the way in which certain churches validate their youth programs. They have felt successful when they have been able to put such a group on the road during Easter vacation week, taking a musical program from church to church.

Young people who didn't think they could sing discover that they can learn some easy, tuneful, rhythmic music—perhaps by singing along with a record just as they learn pop songs. Appropriate instrumentalists—for example, guitarists or drummers—are often easier to find in a small community than competent pianists or organists. The tempo is upbeat. A bit of movement is included. The director need not be skilled in creating choral tone or interpreting traditional musical styles. The customary repertoire of such a group is usually one of the pop-related musicals that encourages an open sharing of faith. All in all, this provides the opportunity for an exciting experience of fellowship, achievement, and a sense of ministry. Participation in such a group has often been the beginning point of a young person's relationship to Christ and his church. Churches and communities too small to generate anything worthwhile in the form of a traditional youth choir have been able to do something useful and satisfying in this idiom.

Nevertheless, there is a negative side to this practice. The principle of diminishing returns sets in. The possibility of doing a second musical is exciting after a first successful experience. However, the prospect of beginning a sixth or seventh is not nearly so attractive. The simplicity of this idiom is both its appeal and its undoing. The music that was so much fun at first loses its excitement. The limited scope of theological ideas and the sameness with which they are expressed becomes boring. The newness of travel, with its inevitable combination of delight and difficulty, wears off. There is a tendency for the whole process to become more and more expensive. Attempts will be made to upgrade the experience with more sophisticated electronic equipment, costumes, and travel arrangements. Increasingly complex choreography may require professional coaching. Occasionally, young people will begin to find that the cost of participation is prohibitive. It gets harder and harder to hold choir members and enlist new ones. The novelty has worn off.

There are a few steps that can be taken to anticipate the inevitable process described above: One must face reality. The evangelical musical cannot, alone, be the basis for the continuing fruitful existence of a youth choir. Musical and spiritual growth must take place, and this medium does not allow for that.

The immediate response, once one is aware of the problem, needs to be the earnest search for musical material that can go beyond the simplistic evangelical statement. This will involve seeking theological breadth as well as textual and musical quality. Such compositions exist, but they are rare.

Beyond this, radical reconsideration will have to be

given to the role of the choir. Young people must be helped to discover satisfaction and a sense of ministry in the less colorful, more mundane task of regularly serving the same congregation. This calls for more than a basic evangelical message because of the reasonable assumption that the majority of the weekly congregation is already committed to Christianity. It will also necessitate the laborious development of musical skills in order to be able to cope adequately with the more traditional choral literature. Emphasis must be placed more and more on the role of the choir as a prompter and servant of the congregation.

One of the consequences of such a change in the understanding of the choir's ministry will be the need for more highly skilled musical leadership. A wider variety of choral techniques will be demanded by the new repertoire and a director must possess a higher level of musical competence to train the singers. Many leaders capable of energizing a group of young people and helping them in doing a pop musical lack this further degree of competence. A readjustment in the expectations of the pastor and the church is called for. In some churches where adequate musical leadership is unavailable, it will be necessary to shift the focus of youth activities from doing such pop musicals to other nonmusical activities.

An alternative to such change of program may be for the church to encourage professional growth on the part of the individual who has become a musical leader by way of the youth musical. Membership in professional societies, participation in choral workshops and conferences, and taking courses in a local college can be the means of such growth. Even as the church expects to support the pastor in continuing education, it should consider its

responsibility for the necessary continuing development
of its musical leaders.

Pop music *has* invaded the church. This invasion has
pushed us to a new understanding of ourselves as the
church and to a new relationship with our environment
—the world. It has offered new possibilities for worship
and outreach, and it has brought its own cluster of problems. Most of all, it has reminded us that the Kingdom
will always need that which is old and that which is new.

A Postscript

"That conversation, understanding, and growth may take place between pastor and musician" was the stated purpose of this book. It would seem appropriate, therefore, to close the book with a chapter on staff relationships. That chapter is missing.

The reason is not an oversight on the part of the author. As I look back over what has been written, I see that this subject has been dealt with consistently. One could say that the whole book is related to this subject. Good relationships within a church staff do not depend upon agreement on every point, but on mutual understanding and appreciation. Each staff member has a distinctive preparation, a peculiar giftedness, and a particular function to perform in the life of the congregation. We have discussed many subjects upon which misunderstandings arise. It is hoped that these discussions will assist both pastors and musicians to identify the nature of these differences and find common ground for dealing with them.

An invitation has been repeatedly offered to worship leaders, particularly pastors and musicians, to face such differences in the context of the basic nature of the church's ministry. "What do we think we are doing in worship?" "What do we want to do?" "Why are we doing what we do?" "What should we be doing?" "What can we do?"

We share the ministry with one another and with God. He has called us to it, and it is his spirit that guides and supports us in it. And most important of all, he may be seeking to teach each of us through the other. Listen for what God is trying to say!

Notes

1. Erik Routley, *Hymns and Human Life* (Philosophical Library, Inc., 1953), p. 307.

2. C. S. Lewis (comp.), *George Macdonald: An Anthology* (The Macmillan Company, 1947), p. 113.

3. Routley, *Hymns and Human Life,* p. 299.

4. John Le Carré, *A Small Town in Germany* (Le Carré Productions, Ltd., 1968).

5. Karl Barth, *The Doctrine of Reconciliation* (*Church Dogmatics,* Vol. IV, Pt. 2), tr. by Geoffrey W. Bromiley (Edinburgh: T. & T. Clark, 1958), pp. 112f.

6. A discussion of the technical factors involved in the construction of hymn texts and hymn tunes can be found in Austin Lovelace, *The Anatomy of Hymnody* (Abingdon Press, 1965); in Erik Routley's two books, *The Music of Christian Hymnody* (London: Independent Press, Ltd., 1957) and *Hymns Today and Tomorrow* (Abingdon Press, 1964); and in the article by Gracia Grindal, "Language, A Lost Craft Among Hymn Writers," *The Hymn,* Vol. 27, No. 2 (April 1976).

7. My source for this figure is the remarkable index of seventy-eight major English-language twentieth-century hymnals compiled by Katharine Smith Diehl, *Hymns and Tunes: An Index* (The Scarecrow Press, Inc., 1966).

8. Samuel Duffield, *English Hymns* (Funk & Wagnalls Co., 1894), p. vi.

9. Dietrich Bonhoeffer, *Life Together*, tr. by John W. Doberstein (London: SCM Press, Ltd., 1954), p. 51.

10. See the several citations of Paul Gerhardt in Dietrich Bonhoeffer's *Letters and Papers from Prison*, ed. by Eberhard Bethge and tr. by Reginald Fuller (London: SCM Press, Ltd., 1967).

11. Some particularly helpful examples of such literature are Albert E. Bailey, *The Gospel in Hymns* (Charles Scribner's Sons, 1951); Ernest Edwin Ryden, *The Story of Christian Hymnody* (Augustana Press, 1959; and three books by Erik Routley: *Hymns and Human Life*, 2d ed. (Wm. B. Eerdmans Publishing Company, 1966); *Hymns and the Faith* (The Seabury Press, Inc., 1956); and *I'll Praise My Maker* (London: Independent Press, Ltd., 1951).

12. Robert M. Stevenson, *Patterns of Protestant Church Music* (Duke University Press, 1953), p. 162.

13. For information concerning the mechanics of this process, see James Sydnor, *The Hymn and Congregational Singing* (John Knox Press, 1960), Chs. 4 and 7.

14. For further information, see Canon Kenneth H. MacDermott, *The Old Church Gallery Minstrels* (London: S.P.C.K. 1948), and Leonard Ellinwood, *The History of American Church Music* (Morehouse-Gorham Company, Inc., 1953), Ch. 3, "Singing Schools and Early Choirs."

15. Søren Kierkegaard, *Purify Your Hearts,* tr. by A. S. Aldworth and W. S. Ferrie (London: The C. W. Daniel Company, Ltd., 1937), p. 147.

16. See note 13.

17. See Rudolf Otto, *The Idea of the Holy,* tr. by John W. Harvey (Oxford University Press, 1958 [1923]); his discussion of silence and the numinous on pp. 68ff., and of silent worship on pp. 210ff.

18. Some suggestions are to be found in John Durham, *Directed Silence* (London: The Faith Press, 1964). This is oriented in terms of the Anglican liturgy but offers suggestions usable in the free church.

19. Krister Stendahl (ed.), *Immortality and Resurrection,* 4 essays by Oscar Cullmann and others (The Macmillan Company, 1965), p. 11.

20. Schleiermacher discusses this process in his *Christmas Eve,* tr. by W. Hastie (Edinburgh: T. & T. Clark, 1890), where he says, "What the word has made clear, the tones of music must make alive" (pp. 26ff.).

21. See "Symbolic Music in the Movies," *Time,* Jan. 17, 1964.

22. I am indebted to Dr. Routley for the use of this terminology and the development of the related ideas.

23. Archibald Davison, *Church Music* (Harvard University Press, 1952), pp. 129ff.

24. Erik Routley, *Church Music and Theology* (Muhlenberg Press, 1960), p. 40.

25. Bonhoeffer, *Life Together*, p. 33.

26. Karl Barth, *The Word of God and the Word of Man*, tr. by Douglas Horton (London: Hodder & Stoughton, Ltd., 1928), p. 106.

27. O. P. Kretzmann, *The Musical Heritage of the Church*, Vol. VI (Concordia Publishing House, 1963), "Faith and Music," p. 5.

28. Karl Barth, *Theology and Church*, tr. by Louise Pettibone Smith (London: SCM Press, Ltd., 1962 [1928]), p. 157.

29. Jaroslav Pelikan, *Fools for Christ* (Fortress Press, 1955), pp. viiff.

30. Abraham H. Maslow, *Religions, Values, and Peak-Experiences* (Ohio State University Press, 1964).

31. Wilfred M. Bailey, *Awakened Worship* (Abingdon Press, 1972).

32. Such a basic text as Peter H. Parkin and Henry R. Humphreys, *Acoustics, Noise, and Buildings* (Frederick A. Praeger, Inc., 1958), presents the issue as being speech vs. music (p. 108) but cannot reflect the thinking of the past two decades on the nature of the church at worship.

33. Sir James Jeans, *Science and Music* (Cambridge: At the University Press, 1961), p. 212.

34. Alec Robertson, *Sacred Music* (London: Max Parrish & Co., Ltd., 1950), p. 71.

35. John Mann Walker, *Better Music in Our Churches* (The Methodist Book Concern, 1923), p. 107.

36. T. Francis Forth, *The Sanctity of Church Music* (London: Century Press, n.d.), p. 144.

37. For specific details of such ventures, see books such as Erik Routley, *Twentieth Century Church Music* (Oxford University Press, Inc., 1964); Harold Myra and Dean Merrill, *Rock, Bach and Superschlock* (A. J. Holman Company, 1972); Kent Schneider, *The Creative Musician in the Church* (West Lafayette, Indiana: Center for Contemporary Celebration), 1976.

38. Sir Richard Terry, *Calvin's First Psalter, 1539* (London: Ernest Benn, Ltd., 1932), pp. iiff.

39. Ulrich S. Leupold (ed.), *Liturgy and Hymns* (*Luther's Works*, Vol. 53) (Fortress Press, 1965), p. 317.

40. Henry Wilder Foote, *Three Centuries of American Hymnody* (The Shoe String Press, Inc., 1961 [1940]), p. 267.

41. C. S. Lewis, *Christian Reflections,* ed. by Walter Hooper (Wm. B. Eerdmans Publishing Company, 1967), p. 94, "On Christian Music."

42. Helmut Thielicke, *The Trouble with the Church,* tr. and ed. by John W. Doberstein (Harper & Row, Publishers, Inc., 1965), p. 86.

43. Nicolas Slonimsky, *Lexicon of Musical Invective* (Coleman-Ross Company, Inc., 1953).